NICHOLAS WRIGHT

Nicholas Wright trained as an actor, and joined the Royal Court Theatre in London as Casting Director before becoming the first Director of the Court's Theatre Upstairs, where he presented an influential programme of new and first-time writing.

From 1975 to 1977 he was joint Artistic Director of the Royal Court. He joined the National Theatre in 1984 as Literary Manager and was an Associate Director of the National until 1998.

His plays include *Treetops* and *One Fine Day* (Riverside Studios), *The Gorky Brigade* (Royal Court), *The Crimes of Vautrin* (Joint Stock), *The Custom of the Country* and *The Desert Air* (both Royal Shakespeare Company), *Cressida* (Almeida Theatre at the Albery), *Mrs Klein* and *Vincent in Brixton* (National Theatre and West End).

His versions of Ibsen's *John Gabriel Borkman* and Chekhov's *Three Sisters* were seen at the National Theatre, and his versions of Pirandello's *Naked* and Wedekind's *Lulu* were premiered at the Almeida Theatre. His opera libretto *The Little Prince* (music by Rachel Portman) was premiered at Houston Grand Opera in 2003 and shown on BBC TV in 2004.

His writing about the theatre includes *99 Plays* – a personal selection from Aeschylus to the present day – and *Changing Stages*, co-written with Richard Eyre.

Other Adaptations in this Series

AFTER MRS ROCHESTER
Polly Teale
Based on the life and work
of Jean Rhys

ANIMAL FARM
Ian Wooldridge
Adapted from George Orwell

ANNA KARENINA
Helen Edmundson
Adapted from Leo Tolstoy

ARABIAN NIGHTS
Dominic Cooke

BEAUTY AND THE BEAST
Laurence Boswell

CINDERELLA
Stuart Paterson

DR JEKYLL AND MR
HYDE
David Edgar
Adapted from Robert Louis
Stevenson

EMMA
Martin Millar &
Doon MacKichan
Adapted from Jane Austen

FAUST *Parts One and Two*
Howard Brenton
Adapted from Goethe

GONE TO EARTH
Helen Edmundson
Adapted from Mary Webb

HANSEL AND GRETEL
Stuart Paterson

JANE EYRE
Polly Teale
Adapted from Charlotte
Brontë

KES
Lawrence Till
Adapted from Barry Hines

MADAME BOVARY
Fay Weldon
Adapted from Gustave
Flaubert

MEDEA
Liz Lochhead
Adapted from Euripides

THE MILL ON THE FLOSS
Helen Edmundson
Adapted from George Eliot

MISERYGUTS &
TARTUFFE
Liz Lochhead
Adapted from Molière

SLEEPING BEAUTY
Rufus Norris

SUNSET SONG
Alastair Cording
Adapted from Lewis Grassic
Gibbon

THEBANS
Liz Lochhead
Adapted from Sophocles
and Euripides

WAR AND PEACE
Helen Edmundson
Adapted from Leo Tolstoy

His Dark Materials

based on the novels by
Philip Pullman

adapted by
Nicholas Wright

NICK HERN BOOKS
London
www.nickhernbooks.co.uk

A Nick Hern Book

This stage adaptation of *His Dark Materials* first published in this revised edition in Great Britain as a paperback original in 2004 by Nick Hern Books Limited, 14 Larden Road, London W3 7ST

First published 2003

His Dark Materials by Nicholas Wright copyright © 2003, 2004 Somerset West Limited

Introduction by Nicholas Wright copyright © 2004 Somerset West Limited

Nicholas Wright has asserted his right to be identified as the author of this work

Front cover image © Jerry Uelsmann (courtesy Laurence Miller Gallery, New York), designed by Michael Mayhew

Typeset by Country Setting, Kingsdown, Kent, CT14 8ES
Printed and bound in Great Britain by Bookmarque, Croydon, Surrey

A CIP catalogue record for this book is available from the British Library

ISBN 1 85459 831 7

Contents

Introduction

When Nicholas Hytner asked me to adapt *His Dark Materials*
for the National Theatre, I said 'yes' without a moment's
hesitation. The first reason was that I had read the books and
loved them. The second was that the dates were fixed, the show
would happen whether I agreed to be part of it or not, and I
thought it would be deeply pathetic to watch the train take off
on its fabulous journey when I could be on it. The third reason
was the nature of the work that I would be doing. Playwrights
like to think that they're the sole author of everything that
happens onstage. But in this case I knew that I would be
sharing the driver's compartment with many others. Like the
book-writer of a big musical, or the screenwriter of a film,
I would be referring constantly to the designer, the movement
director, the composer and every other member of the creative
team. I would be working with the producer and the director,
both united in the form of Nick Hytner. And I would be
working with Philip Pullman. All this was very attractive.

On 2 March 2004, Philip, Nick and I sat in the Olivier Theatre
watching the last performance of the first run. It went incredibly
well and we were all very proud of it. And it occurred to all
three of us that, since we knew the show would come back at
the end of the year, we had the chance to bring it even closer to
the impossible ideal that we had set ourselves when the project
began. This is a luxury that one gets very rarely, and it seemed
crazy not to take advantage of it. It took about five minutes in
the Green Room afterwards for us to say to each other, in
general terms, what we thought was needed. I outlined the
changes that I wanted to make to the script, as well as one or
two others that I wanted to do but wasn't sure how. Philip
promised to help by putting his thoughts in writing, which he
duly did in a long, appreciative and thoughtful letter. Nick, like
every great producer, gave me inspiration, responsibility and
the illusion of freedom.

This revised play-script is the result. It contains a lot of small changes, a few middling ones and one big piece of restructuring in the last half-hour or so. My hopes for it are simple ones: that the story is thrilling, that the great issues that it tackles will excite the imagination of a young audience and that Philip Pullman's central themes of innocence and experience, childhood and adulthood, belief and rationality, will stand out clearly.

Out of the whole experience of the show's creation, these are some of the moments that I will never forget:

The moment at home when I stole a speech from a delightful character in *Northern Lights* named Ma Costa, and gave it to Mrs Coulter: this is when the play began to breathe. The workshop at the National Theatre Studio when Nick turned to me, his eyes ablaze with a kind of white, unearthly energy, and said of the script, 'It's just not working.' The first daemons being unpacked from Michael Curry's Oregon workshop. The way their personalities subverted the room, like ventriloquists' dummies out of a Hoffman story. The first bear coming to life. The first time Lyra's Death appeared. Walking into a rehearsal room, finding it packed with people and being reminded of the Israelites amassed on the shore of the Red Sea, waiting for the miracle that would take them across it. The morning that Giles Cadle showed the cast how the set would work, to half-comprehending wonderment. The first time Jonathan Dove played the music, and the emotional power of the story felt newly unleashed. The first time that we got to the end. And on and on, through previews and opening-day until, finally, a moment in the summer of 2004, the weekend before I was about to deliver this revised script. There was a theme in the play – it doesn't matter which – that I had always known was important but that I had never known how to make sense of. On that Sunday afternoon, a speech arrived from nowhere that gave it meaning. I looked back in my diary and discovered that it was exactly two years to the day since I had started writing: two years of synopses, drafts, workshops and the most exciting rehearsals, because the most dangerous ones, that I had ever experienced.

I was helped and supported for every second of that time. By Nick Hytner, with his optimism, his grasp of the big issues and his ferocious analysis. By the many actors who took part in workshops, rehearsals and performance. Nick Drake read the script in several drafts and gave me excellent advice. Andrew Steggall helped me by compiling a vast concordance of phrases, descriptions and references from the books, and he also came up with some radical thoughts, at least one of which plays a big part in the show.

Finally, Philip Pullman has been supportive at every stage, from the moment that Nick Hytner and I first met him. It must be strange to see your writing being taken over to fit the demands of a different medium. But Philip has always been first to say, 'Don't worry! The books are one thing, and this is another.' And his advice has always led us closer towards a piece of theatre that stands up in its own right, not as a shadow of his stupendous novels.

Nicholas Wright
November 2004

His Dark Materials was first performed in the Olivier Theatre at the National Theatre, London, on 3 January 2004 (previews from 6 December 2003).

The production was revived in a revised version on 8 December 2004 (previews from 20 November), with the following cast:

Part One

Lyra Belacqua	Elaine Symons
Pantalaimon, *her daemon*	Jamie Harding
Will Parry	Michael Legge

OXFORD

Master of Jordan College	David Killick
Professor Hopcraft	Iain Mitchell
Professor Tonkin	Don Gallagher

Lord Asriel	David Harewood
Stelmaria, *his daemon*	Emma Manton
Thorold, *his manservant*	Samuel Roukin

Mrs Coulter	Lesley Manville
The Golden Monkey, *her daemon*	Leo Kay

Fra Pavel, *an emissary from Geneva*   Nick Sampson

Cawson, *Steward of Jordan College*	Alan Perrin
Mrs Lonsdale, *housekeeper*	Vanessa Earl
Roger Parslow, *a kitchen boy*	Darren Hart
Salcilia, *his daemon*	Victoria Moseley
Billy Costa	Marc Bailey
Tony Costa	Harry Peacock

LONDON

Lord Boreal	John Carlisle

Daisy	Helen Murton
Jessie	Michelle Dockery
Lily	Samantha Lawson
Stallholder	Don Gallagher
Top-hatted man	Iain Mitchell
Ben, *Tony Costa's friend*	Pascal Langdale

TROLLESUND

John Faa, *Lord of the Western gyptians*	Ian Gelder
Farder Coram	David Killick
Iorek Byrnison, *an armoured bear*	Alistair Petrie
Bear-keeper	Chiké Okonkwo
Mayor	Don Gallagher
Kaisa, *Serafina's daemon*	Elliot Levey
Lee Scoresby, *a balloonist*	Alistair Petrie
Hester, *his daemon*	Victoria Moseley

BOLVANGAR

Sister Clara	Vanessa Earl
Sister Betty	Rachel Sanders
Dr West	Dodger Phillips
Dr Cade	Chiké Okonkwo
Dr Sargent	Iain Mitchell
Tortured Witch	Samantha Lawson

SVALBARD

Iofur Raknison, *King of armoured bears*	Don Gallagher
Bear Patrol	Ian Gelder
	Pascal Langdale
	Harry Peacock

GENEVA

President of the Consistorial Court	Ian Gelder
Brother Jasper	Elliot Levey
Perpetua, *his daemon*	Victoria Moseley

LAPLAND
Serafina Pekkala, *Queen of the Lapland witches*

	Adjoa Andoh
Ruta Skadi, *Queen of the Latvian witches*	Rachel Sanders
Pipistrelle	Helen Murton
Caitlin	Vanessa Earl
Grimhild	Emma Manton
Grendella	Michelle Dockery

Jopari, *a Shaman*   Iain Mitchell

CITTÀGAZZE
Angelica	Michelle Dockery
Paolo	Marc Bailey
Giacomo Paradisi	David Killick
Tullio	Leo Kay

OXFORD
| Librarian | Samantha Lawson |
| Assistant | Leo Kay |

Part Two

Lyra Belacqua	Elaine Symons
Pantalaimon, *her daemon*	Jamie Harding
Will Parry	Michael Legge

GENEVA
President of the Consistorial Court	Ian Gelder
Brother Jasper	Elliot Levey
Hardball Cleric	Don Gallagher
Softball Cleric	Alistair Petrie
Fervent Cleric	Pascal Langdale
Wily Cleric	David Killick

OXFORD
Lord Boreal	John Carlisle
Mrs Coulter	Lesley Manville
The Golden Monkey, *her daemon*	Leo Kay

CITTÀGAZZE
Serafina Pekkala, *Queen of the Lapland witches*

	Adjoa Andoh
Kaisa, *her daemon*	Elliot Levey
Pipistrelle	Helen Murton
Caitlin	Vanessa Earl
Grimhild	Emma Manton
Grendella	Michelle Dockery

Giacomo Paradisi	David Killick
Angelica	Michelle Dockery
Paolo	Marc Bailey

LORD ASRIEL'S FORTRESS

| Lord Asriel | David Harewood |
| Stelmaria, *his daemon* | Emma Manton |

Lord Roke, *a Gallivespian*	Nick Sampson
The Chevalier Tialys, *a Gallivespian*	Alistair Petrie
Lady Salmakia, *a Gallivespian*	Vanessa Earl

CITTÀGAZZE MOUNTAINS

| Ruta Skadi, *Queen of the Latvian witches* | Rachel Sanders |
| Jopari, *a Shaman* | Iain Mitchell |

| Balthamos, *an angel* | Samuel Roukin |
| Baruch, *an angel* | Pascal Langdale |

NORTHERN MOUNTAINS

| Iorek Byrnison, *an armoured bear* | Alistair Petrie |

OUTSIDE THE LAND OF THE DEAD

Perkins, *an official*	Alan Perrin
Jeptha Jones	Don Gallagher
Hannah, *his wife*	Helen Murton
Old Mother Jones' Death	David Killick
Lyra's Death	Jamie Harding
Boatman	John Carlisle

LAND OF THE DEAD
No-Name, *a harpy*   Rachel Sanders
Harpies   Samantha Lawson
                                      Victoria Moseley
Roger Parslow   Darren Hart

UNKNOWN WORLD
Kirjava, *Will's daemon*   Victoria Moseley

Scholars, students, stolen children, party guests, Trollesunders, witches, clerics, bears, cliff-ghasts, ghosts, Tartar guards and others played by members of the company.

Director   Nicholas Hytner *with* Matt Wilde
Associate Director/Choreographer   Aletta Collins
Set Designer   Giles Cadle
Costume Designer   Jon Morrell
Puppet Designer   Michael Curry
Lighting Designer   Paule Constable
Associate Lighting Designer   Vic Smerdon
Composer   Jonathan Dove
Music Associate   Matthew Scott
Music Director   Mark Bousie
Fight Director   Terry King
Sound Designer   Paul Groothuis
Associate Sound Designer   Matthew Smethurst-Evans
Video Graphics Designers   Thomas Gray and Yuri Tanaka
    for The Gray Circle

Musicians
Mark Bousie (music director/keyboards); David Berry (double bass); Hugh Webb (harp); Joy Hawley (cello); Tracy Holloway (trombone); Philip Hopkins (percussion); Colin Rae (trumpet); Nancy Ruffer (flute).

PART ONE

CHARACTERS IN PART ONE

Between the Worlds

LORD ASRIEL *and* STELMARIA
JOPARI
THOROLD, *Lord Asriel's manservant*

Lyra's World

JORDAN COLLEGE
LYRA BELACQUA *and* PANTALAIMON
ROGER PARSLOW *and* SALCILIA
THE MASTER
PROFESSOR HOPCRAFT
MRS LONSDALE
CAWSON, *a college servant*

LONDON
MRS COULTER *and the* GOLDEN MONKEY
LORD BOREAL
DAISY
JESSIE
LILY
STALLHOLDER
TOP-HATTED MAN

THE CHURCH
THE PRESIDENT
FRA PAVEL
BROTHER JASPER *and* PERPETUA

GYPTIANS
LORD FAA
FARDER CORAM
TONY COSTA
BILLY COSTA
BEN

TROLLESUND
LEE SCORESBY *and* HESTER
MAYOR
BEAR-KEEPER

WITCHES
SERAFINA PEKKALA *and* KAISA
RUTA SKADI
GRIMHILD
PIPISTRELLE
CAITLIN
GRENDELLA

BOLVANGAR
DR SARGENT
DR CADE
DR WEST
NURSE

BEARS
IOREK BYRNISON
IOFUR RAKNISON

Cittàgazze

ANGELICA
PAOLO
GIACOMO PARADISI
TULLIO

Our World

WILL PARRY
LIBRARIAN
LIBRARY ASSISTANT

SCHOLARS, STUDENTS, STOLEN CHILDREN, PARTY
GUESTS, GYPTIANS, TROLLESUNDERS, WITCHES,
CLERICS, BEARS, TARTAR GUARDS, CLIFF-GHASTS
and others

ACT ONE

Oxford / Oxford. The Botanic Gardens. Night. A tree with spreading branches. LYRA *and* WILL, *both aged about twenty, are waiting on a wooden bench.* WILL *has an old green leather writing-case.*

A clock strikes twelve.

LYRA. Will?

WILL. Lyra?

LYRA. This morning I half woke up, and I felt so happy. Even before I knew what day it was. Then I remembered it was Midsummer Day. I looked at the clock and I thought, it's only sixteen hours to midnight. Sixteen hours, and I'll be sitting right next to you.

WILL. I had to scramble over the wall this time. There was a copper on duty till quarter to twelve.

LYRA. I know you're there.

Pause.

WILL. I'm wearing my one good shirt and I've cleaned my trainers. I don't usually look so smart. I'm sharing a house now with three other students, and one of them said, 'Hello, Will, don't tell us you've got a date at last.' I said, 'I do, in fact.' He said, 'Oh, nice one, when do we get to meet her?' I said, 'That might be difficult.'

He laughs, then stops.

I still miss you.

PANTALAIMON. Say something.

WILL. I miss Pantalaimon too. Your daemon. Your soul. I miss him as much as I miss you. Because he *is* you.

PANTALAIMON. Tell him about the college.

WILL. I know he's there. I know *you're* there. Even though you're further away from me than the furthest star . . . you're here. Right here. On the same bench. In a different world.

LYRA. I've had a very good year at college. It's like they told me, all those years ago . . . if I work very hard I can start, just start to do the things that came so naturally to me when I was a kid.

WILL. 'I spread my wings, and I brush ten million other worlds, and they know nothing of it.'

LYRA. It's different for me, from what it's like for the other students. Jordan College is new for them. They see the obvious things, like books and towers and ancient stones. I see the place where I grew up. I see Mrs Lonsdale, who was meant to look after me and keep me tidy . . .

MRS LONSDALE *is there to change* LYRA*'s clothes.*

MRS LONSDALE. Just what do you think you're wearing, Miss Lyra?

LYRA. I see the mouse-holes and the secret doorways, and the hiding-places. And the mouldy old scholars with their flapping gowns. I see Roger, like he was on the day I met him. I was twelve. Me and the other college kids had been fighting the kids from town. Then we all joined up to fight the brick-burners' kids down by the clay-pits. And then we remembered it was the horse-fair week . . . so we all rushed down to the river to fight the gyptian kids. I was fighting Billy Costa.

LYRA*'s Oxford.* WILL *and his world disappear.* LYRA *is twelve. Assorted* KIDS *are yelling at the* GYPTIAN KIDS.

KIDS. Oi! Gyppoes!

Water rats!

Fortune-tellers!

Tea-leaves!

Want any knives sharpened?

Any old iron!

GYPTIAN KIDS *and other* KIDS *fight.* LYRA *gets* BILLY
COSTA *down on the ground in a headlock. The others
clear.*

LYRA. Give up, Billy?

BILLY. No!

LYRA. Now?

BILLY. No!

LYRA. What about now?

BILLY. Yeah! Get off.

They stand.

How'd you do that?

LYRA. It's a headlock. Look, I'll show you.

BILLY. Leave off!

BILLY*'s brother* TONY *appears.*

TONY. Oi, Billy! Our ma says, get back home this minute or
she'll give you a clip.

LYRA. Hello, Tony.

TONY. Don't you 'hello' me, you horrible little tyke. Wasn't it
you throwing mud at our boat just now?

LYRA. That weren't me. It was some other kids.

TONY. Oh yeah!

LYRA. They come down from Abingdon in a special coach . . .
all painted black, with a skeleton driving. And he saw your
boat, and he pointed his bony finger . . .

TONY. Oh aye. Lyra the liar. En't that what they call you? Go
on, get back home. Come on, Billy.

He and BILLY *go.* LYRA *stays, dejected.* ROGER *runs on.*

ROGER. Where's the fighting?

LYRA. You missed it.

ROGER. Who won?

LYRA. Dunno. Don't matter either. See yer, whoever you are.

ROGER. See yer.

They turn to go.

PANTALAIMON. I'm Pantalaimon.

SALCILIA. I'm Salcilia.

PANTALAIMON. I en't seen you before.

SALCILIA. That's 'cause we only just arrived from London.

The DAEMONS *approach each other.* LYRA *and* ROGER *look at them in surprise.*

ROGER. That's funny.

LYRA. They wanna be friends.

ROGER. That could be. My mum always says, you know at once when you like somebody. An' I like you. I'm Roger. Roger Parslow. My dad's the new head gardener at Gabriel College, an' me mum's a cook an' I'm gonna be a kitchen boy.

LYRA. I'm Lyra Belacqua an' I'm at Jordan College. I don't work there or nothing. I just play around.

ROGER. Jordan's bigger'n Gabriel, en't it?

LYRA. It's bigger an' richer an' ever so much more important. You wanna see it?

ROGER. Yeah, don't mind.

LYRA. Come on, then.

They walk on.

ROGER. Where's *your* mum an' dad?

LYRA. En't got none. I'm nearly an orphan.

ROGER. You can't be *nearly* an orphan.

LYRA. You can if you're me. I got an uncle, and he's famous.

ROGER. Bet I never heard of 'im.

LYRA. Bet you have.

ROGER. So what's his name?

LYRA. Lord Asriel.

ROGER. *Him*? What, the explorer an' all?

LYRA. That's right.

ROGER. Well, that *is* famous. What's he like?

LYRA. He's old, like . . . forty at least. And he's *ferocious*.
There was some Tartars caught him once, and they tied him
up, and one of 'em was just gonna cut his guts out, and
Lord Asriel looked at him – just looked, like that – and he
dropped down dead.

PANTALAIMON. Lyra the liar!

LYRA. It was summat like that.

They have arrived at Jordan College. A couple of
STUDENTS *cycle past.* SCHOLARS *are circulating. The*
MASTER *appears with* FRA PAVEL.

Right, this is the quad, an' underneath us there's the crypt,
with tunnels windin' everywhere like a 'normous sponge.
An' those are the scholars, an' that's the Master of the
College.

ROGER. Who's that snakey feller who's picking his nose?

LYRA. That's Fra Pavel. He comes to look at me twice a year
and asks me questions.

MASTER. Lyra, one moment.

LYRA *approaches.*

Fra Pavel is here. He arrived this morning from the
Consistorial Court of Discipline in Geneva to inspect your
progress.

FRA PAVEL. Good evening, Lyra.

LYRA (*guarded*). 'Ello.

FRA PAVEL. Are you still happy at Jordan College?

LYRA. Sort of.

FRA PAVEL. Do you learn your lessons? Do you say your prayers to the Authority?

LYRA. Mm hm.

FRA PAVEL. Have you decided what you will do, once you've grown up and your daemon is settled?

LYRA. I'll go exploring with Lord Asriel. He's gonna take me up the Amazon river, or into the desert, or the Arctic Circle . . .

FRA PAVEL. Is this true?

MASTER. No, not at all. You surely remember her weakness for fantastic stories. Your uncle is far too busy to see you when he comes to Jordan College, isn't he, Lyra?

LYRA. But he's coming on Wednesday week. Mrs Lonsdale told me. And he'll see me then, I'm gonna make sure he does. I'll follow him round, till . . .

FRA PAVEL (*to* LYRA). Play with your friend.

LYRA *goes.*

Why was I not informed of Lord Asriel's visit?

MASTER. I would have warned you, if you'd given me time. Lord Asriel has offered to show us the findings of his latest expedition to the Arctic. Some of the scholars are most enthusiastic. Others, of course, are as shocked as you. I try to steer a moderate course, but . . .

FRA PAVEL. There *is* no moderate course. You are either for the Church or you're against it. Don't you *see* that? Don't you know what's happening outside your smug little ivory tower? Fears of war. Rebellion. Dissent, confusion, schism, doubt. All fuelled by the mad ambitions of Lord Asriel and the complacency of academics like yourself.

MASTER. Then what must I do?

FRA PAVEL. Since that heretic has been foolish enough to place himself in your hands, you must take advantage of it. You must render him harmless, by the most extreme of measures. Is that agreed?

MASTER. No, certainly not! Or only if . . . though, on the other hand . . . I'll do as you say. But under protest.

FRA PAVEL. Let's walk on.

They do.

Lyra has changed. I see in her both the child she is, and the woman she will become.

MASTER. Is anything wrong with that?

FRA PAVEL. Time will tell.

They go.

Two weeks later. Oxford. Evening. SCHOLARS *appear, and continue to assemble.* LYRA *and* ROGER *enter.*

LYRA. He's here, Pan. He's here!

1ST SCHOLAR (*to* LYRA). Out of the quad! Out of the quad! He's here! Look, there's his zeppelin!

They look.

2ND SCHOLAR. I do believe he's going to moor it to the roof of the chapel.

3RD SCHOLAR. Disgraceful.

5TH SCHOLAR. Rather amusing, though!

4TH SCHOLAR (*who is very old*). Is something happening?

1ST SCHOLAR. Yes, Lord Asriel's just arrived.

4TH SCHOLAR. What did he say?

Someone explains as:

1ST SCHOLAR. We'll exchange a few polite formalities, and then we'll take him through to dinner in the Great Hall.

2ND SCHOLAR. Look! He's getting out!

6TH SCHOLAR. Professor Hopcraft has arrived.

HOPCRAFT. Gentlemen, gentlemen! What's going on? It's not a *welcoming* party, surely?

3RD SCHOLAR. We mustn't let Lord Asriel think that we approve of him.

1ST SCHOLAR. Well, some of us do.

Disagreement breaks out, as:

5TH SCHOLAR. The Master's gone to greet him, so he can't be totally in disgrace.

THOROLD *appears, followed by a college servant,* CAWSON, *who is carrying equipment.*

2ND SCHOLAR. There's his manservant.

SEVERAL. Welcome, Thorold!

THOROLD. Evening, gentlemen.

1ST SCHOLAR. The lecture is in the Retiring Room, just behind the Lodge.

THOROLD. I en't forgotten my way, sir. Mind that box, Mr Cawson, there's glass inside it.

He goes.

1ST SCHOLAR. I hear that Lord Asriel is going to give us a magic-lantern show.

HOPCRAFT. Is he? Really? Doesn't that smack of entertainment?

The MASTER *appears.*

MASTER. Our guest is here.

LORD ASRIEL *enters with his snow-leopard daemon,* STELMARIA. *There's a ripple of applause from the*

SCHOLARS, *who shake his hand while greetings are exchanged.* LYRA *tries hard to attract his attention.*

LORD ASRIEL (*to a* SCHOLAR). Professor Tonkin, I hear your book's been a great success.

LYRA. Hello!

LORD ASRIEL *ignores her, and the* MASTER *bustles her aside.*

MASTER. Out of the way!

LORD ASRIEL (*to another*). Congratulations on your professorship, Richard.

LYRA *is back.*

LYRA. It's me!

MASTER. Now then, Lyra!

She is shunted out of the way.

LORD ASRIEL. Professor Hopcraft, may I say how much I admire your writing?

HOPCRAFT (*charmed*). Oh, you've read it? Well, I'm flattered. Though I . . .

MASTER. Shall we go to the dining hall, My Lord?

LYRA *and* ROGER *watch as they all go.*

ROGER. He's awesome.

She starts to go.

Hey, where you goin'?

LYRA. Where d'you think? We're gonna sneak into the Retiring Room while they're still having their dinner. I know a secret way.

PANTALAIMON. Lyra, we can't! It en't just any old room.

SALCILIA. Kids can't go in there, and nor can women.

PANTALAIMON. Yeah, and it's probably haunted.

LYRA. Good, that settles it. Come on, Rodge, this is gonna be fun.

They go.

The Retiring Room appears. THOROLD *and* CAWSON *are there,* CAWSON *setting down a tray with glasses and a decanter.*

CAWSON. This wine is for Lord Asriel's pleasure only. It's the 1898.

THOROLD. That's very thoughtful of the Master. It's His Lordship's favourite year. After you, Mr Cawson.

They go. LYRA *and* ROGER *appear through a secret doorway. They look round.*

LYRA. Wow.

ROGER. It's spooky all right.

PANTALAIMON. This is a bad idea.

ROGER *finds the projector.*

ROGER. 'Ere, look.

SALCILIA. Don't touch it!

ROGER. I won't break it.

He looks.

'Ere, Lyra, come an' look. This is fancy.

LYRA *is looking at the walls.*

LYRA. I wanna look at them paintings. All the Masters with their daemons.

PANTALAIMON. Now that *is* interesting.

LYRA. He's got a falcon daemon.

PANTALAIMON. He's got a magpie.

LYRA. That one's got an owl. He must have been specially clever.

A bell is heard.

They've finished dinner! Let's go back in here. Pan, Salcilia, change into something small.

The DAEMONS *change into moths.* LYRA *and* ROGER *hide. The* MASTER *comes in. He looks round and, having established that the room is empty, takes a small phial from his pocket, empties it into the decanter and creeps out.* LYRA *and* ROGER *appear.*

He poisoned the wine!

ROGER. How d'you know it's poison?

LYRA. It must be. Why else did he look around like that, all furtive-like?

PANTALAIMON. You can't jump out and make a fuss, we'll get into trouble.

LYRA. I can't let Lord Asriel be murdered, Pan!

ROGER. Shuddup! He's here!

LORD ASRIEL *comes in with* STELMARIA *and* THOROLD, *who adjusts the projection equipment.* LYRA *and* ROGER *get out of sight.* PANTALAIMON *and* SALCILIA *watch.*

LORD ASRIEL. Is everything set up?

THOROLD. It is, sir.

LORD ASRIEL. Excellent. The sooner I can get out of this place, the better.

CAWSON *comes in with a cup of coffee on a tray.*

CAWSON. Good evening, My Lord.

LORD ASRIEL. Good evening, Cawson. Is that the college Tokay I can see on the table?

CAWSON. It is, sir. There are only three bottles left in the cellars. The Keeper of Wine was somewhat taken aback, but the Master was most particular.

THOROLD. Thank you, Mr Cawson.

> CAWSON *and* THOROLD *go.* LORD ASRIEL *goes to pour wine.* LYRA *watches in great suspense.*

LORD ASRIEL. Smell the air. Must, fust and dry bones. Nothing has changed. Nothing is new. I'd like to smash those windows and let some air in.

STELMARIA. You're tired. You ought to be resting.

LORD ASRIEL. I know, I know. And I ought to have changed my clothes. There's probably some ancient etiquette that allows them to fine me half a swan and a bottle of claret for being improperly dressed.

> *He is about to drink.*

LYRA. No!

LORD ASRIEL. Who's there!

LYRA. Don't drink it!

> *She scrambles forward to snatch the glass from his hand.*

LORD ASRIEL. Lyra! What are you doing in here?

LYRA. Throw it away! It's poisoned.

LORD ASRIEL. What did you say?

LYRA. I saw the Master pouring something into it.

LORD ASRIEL. The *Master*?

LYRA. Yeah. I was hiding in there, an' . . .

> LORD ASRIEL *sees* ROGER.

LORD ASRIEL. Who's that?

LYRA. That's Roger. He's my best friend. 'Ere, Rodge . . . !

LORD ASRIEL. Stay where you are, young man. One bothersome child is quite enough. (*To* LYRA.) Why were you hiding?

LYRA. I wanted to see you. I wanted to ask you when you'd take me to the Arctic, so I'd . . .

LORD ASRIEL. Don't be ridiculous. You're a child.

LYRA. But . . .

LORD ASRIEL. Don't argue with me. I have to get back to the Arctic and I don't have any money. That's why I'm here. I'm trying to get the college to pay for the expedition, and they don't know that yet. Go away. No, stop. Let me look at you.

He looks at her.

You seem healthy enough. Show me your hands.

She does.

Disgusting. Where do you play, to get so dirty?

LYRA. In the clay-pits. An' up on the roofs. Rodge an' me found a rook up there. It'd hurt its foot. I was gonna cook it an' eat it, but Rodge said we oughta make it better, so we gave it some wine and some bits of food, an' . . .

THOROLD *is at the door.*

THOROLD. The scholars are here, My Lord.

LORD ASRIEL (*to* LYRA). Here are five gold dollars for you. Get back where you were. Go on!

LYRA *hides. The* MASTER *comes in, followed by* SCHOLARS, *and is astonished to see* LORD ASRIEL *standing with the decanter in his hand.*

MASTER. Lord Asriel!

LORD ASRIEL. Wrong vintage, Master. Thorold, would you mind turning down the lamps?

THOROLD *does, and the* SCHOLARS *take their seats.* LORD ASRIEL *begins.*

Before I show you what I found in the Arctic, I'm going to explain to you why I went there. I was a student here at Jordan College. Some of you taught me. I was young, I was rebellious, and I longed with all my heart to find the answers to those questions that have baffled experimental theologians for centuries. And I still do. Let's start with daemons. Each of us has one.

There's a nonplussed reaction from the HUMANS, *but their* DAEMONS *show great interest.*

We can't imagine a world without them. But what do we really know about our daemons? What do they know about us?

STELMARIA. No more than you.

LORD ASRIEL. Exactly. Isn't it time that we knew . . . let's say . . . why they reflect our natures in the way they do? Why is Stelmaria a snow-leopard while the Master's daemon is a raven? Why are our daemons fixed in one particular shape? Why can't they change?

3RD SCHOLAR (*stating the obvious*). Because we're adults!

LORD ASRIEL. Yet a child's daemon can change whenever it wants to. Why's that? Why can't we touch each others' daemons? Why, if some lunatic were to pull Stelmaria and me apart, would both she and I suffer such agony? And why, if we were separated, would we die? I've done years of research and experiment on this very question, and it seems to me now that the answer lies in that mysterious substance . . . or power . . . or essence . . . that all of us know about, and that none of us truly understands. I mean the elementary particles that we call . . . Dust.

HOPCRAFT *springs up.*

HOPCRAFT. I understood that talk about Dust was not allowed. What is Fra Pavel's view?

MASTER. Fra Pavel is in Geneva. But he told me before he left, that we should watch our tongues.

HOPCRAFT. Then we could all be in very deep water indeed . . .

LORD ASRIEL *overrides him.*

LORD ASRIEL. *This*, gentlemen, is why I went to the Arctic: to find the man who knows more about Dust than anyone else alive: a certain spirit-diviner, an occultist, a *shaman* as he's known to the Northern tribesmen. His name is Jopari. This is a photogram that I took of him on the day we met.

A slide comes up of JOPARI *standing in the moonlight in the snow, beside a hut, with one hand raised.*

There he stands, one hand raised up in greeting. The photogram I shall show you next was taken from the same position a moment later, by a secret process that Jopari taught me. It uses, instead of the normal emulsion, an amber liquid that reveals those things that cannot be seen by the naked eye.

A slide comes up of the same scene, but with a fountain of sparks streaming from JOPARI's *raised hand. The* SCHOLARS *gasp in astonishment.*

Dust is bathing him in radiance. Just as it does to all of us, every moment of our adult lives. But with us, that radiance is invisible. Here, for the first time in human history, we can see it. Here at last we have a clue to the nature of Dust. Where does it come from? The picture seems to show it streaming down from the sky. Is that the answer? But why has it collected around the spirit-diviner in such vast quantity? Has it recognised his special gifts? Has Dust an intelligence?

Animated conversation breaks out between the SCHOLARS.

MASTER. Gentlemen, please!

LORD ASRIEL. And it was this that led me to the most extraordinary discovery of all. Here is a photogram of the Aurora Borealis, which I took in the old-fashioned way.

A slide comes up of the Aurora Borealis.

4TH SCHOLAR. Forgive my ignorance, but if I ever knew what the Aurora was, I have forgotten. Is it the Northern Lights?

LORD ASRIEL. It is. But by using Jopari's secret process, I revealed something I could hardly believe myself.

A second slide appears, looking much the same as the previous one.

3RD SCHOLAR. It's just the same.

1ST SCHOLAR. No . . . there's something different in the centre.

2ND SCHOLAR. Lord Asriel, could you enlarge it, please?

LORD ASRIEL *does. A city appears in the Aurora.*

LORD ASRIEL. We see a . . . city! Towers, domes, walls, buildings, streets, even a line of palm trees . . . suspended in the air . . . all clearly visible through the boundaries of the world we know.

5TH SCHOLAR. Are you saying this city is outside our world?

LORD ASRIEL. It's in a *different* world! Think what that means. If Dust can travel from world to world, then so can light. If light can travel, then so can we. The doors are open to us. The chains are broken. We can question everything we've been taught. We can challenge every dreary, grey belief that we've had dinned into our skulls. Our reach is infinite, and I shall prove it. I shall go back to the Arctic. I'll find the Aurora. I'll build a pathway through its heart into this different world, and I'll cross into it! Will this college support me?

HOPCRAFT. Certainly not. This is blatant support for a highly dangerous theory . . .

SCHOLARS. Name it! / What theory?

HOPCRAFT. I mean the multi-world theory, as you, Professor Chalker, very well know!

1ST SCHOLAR. I propose that we grant Lord Asriel a handsome subvention from the college funds.

SCHOLARS. Hear hear!

The MASTER *springs up.*

MASTER. Lord Asriel, you have gone too far!

LORD ASRIEL. Put it to the vote.

6TH SCHOLAR. All in favour?

Most SCHOLARS *raise their hands.*

3RD SCHOLAR. Those against?

A few SCHOLARS *raise their hands.*

MASTER. The motion is carried.

The meeting breaks up in pandemonium.

3RD SCHOLAR. Dust is evil! Dust is the mark of sin!

ANTI. The Church has put three centuries of thought into this
very question, and I really do think that we have to accept
its judgement. / We ought to be fighting Dust, not talking
about it. / Lord Asriel has been a menace to Jordan College
ever since I knew him as an undergraduate. / The Church
will make a stink and close down our research programmes. /
Who says those photograms are real? They don't look real
to me. They could all be a fake. (*Etc.*)

PRO. I've known for *years* and *years* that the multi-world
theory is solid fact but . . . / Well, the camera doesn't lie. It
doesn't. Really it doesn't. I mean, we've seen the palm trees
and the city and all the rest of it . . . / My students think I'm
a boring old fossil because I cannot admit the truth. / *What*
did you say? *What* did you say? (*Etc.*)

Six weeks later. Jordan College. Day, outside. LYRA, ROGER,
PANTALAIMON *and* SALCILIA. LYRA *is downcast.*

ROGER. Cheer up.

LYRA. I can't. It's six weeks gone since Lord Asriel went to
the Arctic, an' he en't never wrote nor nothing.

ROGER. I thought you said he never does.

LYRA. But it's different this time, en't it? I saved his life.
You'd think a postcard wouldn't be too much bother.

PANTALAIMON. Or a carrier pigeon.

ROGER. It were something though, weren't it? All them
scholars standing on chairs an' shouting . . .

LYRA. . . . and the man with his hand held up. You know what, Rodge?

ROGER. No, what?

LYRA. If I go to the Arctic . . . *when* I go . . . I'm gonna take you with me.

ROGER. I never thought no different.

MRS LONSDALE *appears.*

MRS LONSDALE. There you are. Lyra, you're to come with me and visit the Master. No time to wash, we'll have to make do with hankie and spit.

She does.

LYRA. I don't wanna see him!

ROGER. He's a poisoner!

MRS LONSDALE. What are you talking about, you two? He's a lovely, kind old gentleman who wouldn't say boo to a goose. There, that's better.

They walk on.

And never again let me find you out and about without no grown-ups.

LYRA. Why not?

MRS LONSDALE. Why not? 'Cause it's not safe any more, that's why. There's kids being stolen away in broad daylight, not that anyone knows who's taking 'em.

LYRA. It's the Gobblers take 'em.

MRS LONSDALE. Yes, but who's the Gobblers? That's the question.

ROGER. My dad says there en't no Gobblers. He says it's all got up by the papers.

MRS LONSDALE. Well, he's wrong, quite wrong. There's Gobblers all over the country.

LYRA. But there en't none in Oxford, is there, Mrs Lonsdale?

MRS LONSDALE. I'm afraid there is. I didn't want to upset you, but you'll hear about it soon enough. Young Billy Costa's gone.

LYRA. What, Billy my mate?

ROGER. How did it happen?

MRS LONSDALE. It was just like *that*. He was holding a horse for his brother Tony, and Tony took his eye off him just for a minute, and when he looked back, Billy had vanished.

LYRA. Isn't nobody gonna look for him?

MRS LONSDALE. The gyptians will, 'cause they look after their own. But us landlopers won't be bothering, sad to say. Here we are.

They have arrived at the MASTER*'s study.*

ROGER. Don't drink nothing he gives you.

LYRA. Yeah, and you wait outside and listen, and if I scream for help, you gotta come running in.

The MASTER*'s study.* MRS LONSDALE *knocks on the door.*

MASTER. Come.

LYRA and MRS LONSDALE *go in. The* MASTER *is there.*

MRS LONSDALE. No one keeping an eye on her, Master, and the Gobblers in Oxford, too.

MASTER. Thank you, Mrs Lonsdale.

She goes.

Sit down, Lyra.

LYRA *does.*

You have been in the care of Jordan College for twelve years now, ever since you were brought here as a baby. We are fond of you, you've never been a bad child and you've been happy, I think, in your own way. But that part of your life has ended.

LYRA. What do you mean?

MASTER. A very well-known and distinguished person has offered to take you away.

LYRA. You mean Lord Asriel?

MASTER. No! Lord Asriel cannot communicate with anyone.

LYRA. Is he dead?

MASTER. No, certainly not. He went to the Arctic, as you know, and I have reason to believe he's safe. Now, as for you. There is a friend of the college, a wealthy widow, who has offered to take you to live with her in London.

LYRA. I don't want no bloody widow! I wanna stay here!

MASTER. Lyra . . .

MRS COULTER *appears: a beautiful woman wearing a long yellow-red fox-fur coat. Her daemon is a* GOLDEN MONKEY.

MRS COULTER. May I speak to her?

MASTER. Certainly, Mrs Coulter. This is Lyra.

MRS COULTER *looks at her.*

LYRA. What you lookin' at?

MRS COULTER. You. I haven't seen you since . . . well, ever. And you're just as they described you. Do you like chocolatl? I think I have some in my bag.

LYRA *receives the chocolatl with a show of indifference.*

I know how nervous you must be feeling. I'm a little nervous myself, believe it or not. It's just so . . . very strange to meet you. But we'll take it gently, just to begin with. And we'll soon be friends.

LYRA. I've got a friend. I play with him all the time.

MRS COULTER *turns questioningly to the* MASTER.

MASTER. He's a college serving-boy. His name is Roger.

MRS COULTER. A college servant? Well, I mustn't interfere.
    I'm sure that whatever I say to her, she'll do the opposite.

LYRA. Yes, I will.

MRS COULTER (*laughs. To* LYRA). That is *exactly* what
    I would have said myself, at your age. But seriously, Lyra,
    don't you think you're getting a little too grown-up for
    rough-and-tumble games with boys from a different
    background? You'll be a young woman soon, and . . . let me
    look at you properly . . . yes, you could be a very pretty
    one. Wouldn't you like that?

LYRA. What, just being pretty all day?

MRS COULTER. Oh, more than that. You'll be my personal
    assistant.

MASTER. Mrs Coulter is the Chief Executive Officer of a very
    significant organisation.

LYRA. What's it called?

MRS COULTER. It's called the General Oblation Board.

LYRA. What's an Obla . . . Oblacious?

MASTER. The word 'oblate', Lyra, dates from the Middle
    Ages, when parents would present their children to the
    Church to be monks or nuns. It means a sacrifice, a giving
    away of something precious . . .

    MRS COULTER *silences him with a look.*

MRS COULTER. Let's not confuse her, Master. (*To* LYRA.)
    All that you need to know for now, is that the General
    Oblation Board is a charitable research foundation that finds
    out all about Dust. Have you heard about Dust?

LYRA. I have, yeah . . . but I thought we wasn't supposed to
    talk about it.

MRS COULTER. You can if you have permission. And the
    Church has given the General Oblation Board its total

backing. I shall want you to meet my clients, keep my
appointment book . . . you'd like that, wouldn't you?

It's clear that LYRA *wouldn't.*

There'll be my travel arrangements too, of course. I travel
a great deal.

LYRA. Where to?

MRS COULTER. The Arctic, mostly. I have some very
interesting projects in that part of the world.

LYRA. Would I come with you?

MRS COULTER. Do you want to?

LYRA *disguises her eagerness.*

LYRA. I didn't say that. I'm just asking.

MRS COULTER *changes tack.*

MRS COULTER. Well, one could *make* it a part of your job,
I suppose . . . but I wonder how much you'd really enjoy
it . . . flying in a zeppelin . . . watching the icebergs floating
past us, miles below . . . wouldn't it be too adventurous for
you?

LYRA. No, but . . . No, it wouldn't.

MRS COULTER. And once we get there, there'll be lots of
dreadfully dangerous creatures . . . witches, hungry cliff-
ghasts, armoured bears . . . the bravest fighters on earth, but
oh, so frightening . . . you wouldn't like meeting one of
them, I'm sure.

LYRA. I might not mind.

MRS COULTER. But now I think of it . . . isn't there someone
very special in the Arctic? Someone you'd like to see, who
I could take you to?

LYRA. Do you know Lord Asriel?

MRS COULTER. I know him *very* well. So . . . will you come
to London?

LYRA *hesitates.*

MASTER. The truth is, Lyra, that neither you nor I can choose where we wish to go. We are moved by tides much fiercer than you can imagine, and they sweep us all into the current.

MRS COULTER. Thank you, Master, you've been extremely helpful. I shall inform Geneva. Good night, Lyra. We'll leave in the morning.

LYRA. In the morning?

MRS COULTER *hugs her.*

MRS COULTER. Dear child! We're going to have such fun! (*To the* MASTER.) Good night.

She goes. LYRA *is about to follow her.*

MASTER. One moment, Lyra. Were you by any chance concealed in the Retiring Room, the night Lord Asriel spoke to the scholars?

LYRA. I might have been.

MASTER. So you have reason to mistrust me.

LYRA. Yeah, I do.

MASTER. You must understand, a man in my position has to commit some harm from time to time, in order to prevent some greater evil. But one can try to make up for it. There will be dangers where you are going. You will need protection. I am giving you this.

He produces a small package wrapped in black velvet, and unwraps it to reveal a small, gold, compass-like object.

LYRA. What is it?

MASTER. It is an alethiometer. It was constructed in Prague three hundred years ago. Only six were ever made, and even fewer survive. Lord Asriel presented this one to the college when he was young.

LYRA. What does it do?

MASTER. It tells the truth. But it does so in a way so deep and so mysterious that adults need a whole library of reference books to understand it.

LYRA. What about children?

MASTER. Who can say? Innocence can be wiser than experience. If you could read it, Lyra, even if only a very little, it would be the greatest treasure you ever possessed. Respect it. Keep it safe. Tell no one you have it.

LYRA. Not even Mrs Coulter?

MASTER (*emphatically*). Not even her. Now take it and go.

LYRA *takes the alethiometer and goes into the night outside.*

LYRA. Roger! Roger!

MRS LONSDALE *appears, carrying a lantern.*

Oh, Mrs Lonsdale. Have you seen Roger?

MRS LONSDALE. No, I haven't. Nobody has. They can't find him anywhere.

LYRA. What?

MRS LONSDALE. He was standing here. Right here. I told him he ought to go home. And now the Gobblers have taken him. Oh, that stupid, stupid boy!

LYRA. How can you say that? Don't you care about Roger?

MRS LONSDALE. People care about things in different ways, Miss Lyra. We don't all show it. Roger's my nephew.

LYRA. I didn't know.

MRS LONSDALE. You didn't know because you never asked. He was waiting for *you*.

She moves away, peering into the darkness.

LYRA. He's gone.

PANTALAIMON. Salcilia too.

LYRA. Can you feel it, Pan? It's like I'm only half of meself, and the other half's just . . . not there.

PANTALAIMON. You still got me.

LYRA. Yeah.

She hugs PANTALAIMON.

I'd die if I didn't. And you know what, Pan? Whatever they've done to Roger, wherever they've taken him . . . we're gonna find him. We're gonna rescue him. I swear it.

A bleak collection-point. A brazier is burning. Children are waiting, with suitcases by their sides. Among them are DAISY, JESSIE *and* LILY. *They have all just finished writing letters.* BILLY COSTA *is there. An old* SERVANT *hands round mugs of hot chocolatl.* ROGER *appears.*

ROGER. 'Ello.

SEVERAL. 'Ello.

BILLY. Rodge! 'Ello!

ROGER. 'Ello, Billy.

BILLY. Come an' sit down. (*To the* CHILD *beside him.*) Move up, willya?

He catches the SERVANT'*s eye and points to* ROGER.

Oi, Miss. Don't forget the new boy.

ROGER *sits by him. The* SERVANT *gives* ROGER *a mugful of chocolatl. Meanwhile:*

'Ere, Ratter. You know Roger. Say 'ello.

RATTER, *his daemon, turns away.*

Nah, she's gloomy today.

ROGER. Billy . . .

BILLY. Yeah?

ROGER. . . . 'ave we been taken by the Gobblers?

BILLY. Sure 'ave, mate.

ROGER. What they gonna do to us?

BILLY. Nothin' nasty.

The other CHILDREN *chip in, trying to keep up their spirits.*

DAISY. We all gotta write letters to our mums and dads. In case they're worried about us, know what I mean?

JESSIE. Catch mine getting worried.

ROGER. Is it all right, then? Being a Gobbler-victim?

DAISY. Yeah, it's nice.

JESSIE. We're getting to like it, en't we, Lily?

LILY. We're goin' on a boat.

ROGER. A *boat*? Where to?

LILY. Dunno, but it's gotta be more excitin' than being at 'ome.

JESSIE. I hope it's somewhere 'ot.

LILY. Yeah, with long white beaches.

JESSIE. Or a swimmin' pool!

They all laugh.

DAISY. Ssh! Look be'ind you.

She indicates the tail of the GOLDEN MONKEY, *which has appeared somewhere.* MRS COULTER *appears.*

MRS COULTER. Have you finished your letters, children?

CHILDREN. Yes, miss.

MRS COULTER. Hold them out.

They do, and she collects them.

Have you all been given a suitcase?

CHILDREN. Yes, miss.

MRS COULTER. And your pyjamas? Nighties? Toothbrushes?

CHILDREN. Yes, miss!

MRS COULTER. And who likes chocolatl?

CHILDREN. Me! Me!

MRS COULTER. Well, I happen to know that they'll be handing some out to you the minute you get on board.

CHILDREN. Hooray!

The GOLDEN MONKEY *attracts* MRS COULTER*'s attention.*

MRS COULTER. What?

He points out ROGER.

ROGER. Who, me?

MRS COULTER. Oh dear, you didn't have time to write. But I can give your mother a message.

ROGER. Will you tell her . . .

MRS COULTER. Yes?

ROGER. . . . . to feed my budgie?

MRS COULTER. Isn't there something more important?

ROGER. Just say I love her.

MRS COULTER. She'll be so happy to hear that!

A ship's hooter blows. A door opens and a SEA CAPTAIN *appears. The* CHILDREN *file out.*

Form a line . . . that's right . . . There'll be a nurse to look after you . . . make sure you tell her if you're feeling seasick . . . Ladies first, Billy . . . No pushing each other on the gangplank. Goodbye!

The last CHILDREN *to leave wave and call 'Goodbye!'* MRS COULTER *gives the letters to the* GOLDEN MONKEY *and leaves. He burns the letters.*

MRS COULTER's *living room.* LYRA, *prettily dressed, is admiring herself in a mirror.*

LYRA (*to* PANTALAIMON). I en't never been pretty before. Never in all my life. I en't never had my hair done proper, and my nails all pink and polished.

PANTALAIMON. She's just turning you into a pet.

LYRA. She loves me, though, I'm sure she does. She sits on the end of my bed when she thinks I'm asleep, and she looks at me, so sad, with those big dark eyes.

PANTALAIMON. If she's so good, then why's she got such a horrible, evil daemon?

LYRA. I dunno. But I know what you mean. It's like she's evil and good all at the same time.

She takes out the alethiometer.

PANTALAIMON. What you doin'?

LYRA. I'm gonna have one more go at finding Roger before she comes barging in. I been thinking. If I point the needles at the pictures round the outside . . . maybe that's part of asking the question.

PANTALAIMON *looks.*

PANTALAIMON. Point one of 'em at the moon.

LYRA. Why the moon?

PANTALAIMON. Because it disappears like Roger did.

LYRA. Yeah, right. And the horse, for travel. And . . . what stands for 'Roger'?

PANTALAIMON. Something to do with 'friend'.

LYRA. The dolphin, 'cause dolphins are friendly.

The needles are all in place.

PANTALAIMON. Go on.

LYRA. 'Where's Roger?'

They watch.

PANTALAIMON. That needle's moving.

LYRA. Yeah! But it's not saying nothing, is it? It's just
swinging around any old how. (*Louder.*) 'Where's Roger?'
Oh Pan, it's stopped!

PANTALAIMON. Look out.

The GOLDEN MONKEY *appears, followed by* MRS
COULTER. LYRA *sneaks the alethiometer back into her
shoulder-bag.*

MRS COULTER. Lyra dear, you haven't been out, I hope?

LYRA. No, I been in *all day*!

MRS COULTER. I know I'm always saying this, and I'm sure
you must find it very boring of me, but if you want to go
out, you must do so with me or . . .

LYRA / MRS COULTER. . . . with one of the servants.

MRS COULTER. Exactly.

She rearranges flowers in a vase.

Now are you quite clear about what I want you to do at the
party this evening?

LYRA. I en't forgo'en.

MRS COULTER. *Haven't* forgotten! Sound those 't's. 'T', 't',
't'. I want you to circulate with the canapés and make
agreeable conversation. There'll be some very important
people here . . . friends of mine, and people in government
and opinion-formers . . . and you must live up to their
expectations.

LYRA. They don't know nothin' about me.

MRS COULTER. One can be better known than one is aware
of.

LYRA. How?

MRS COULTER. Stop asking pointless questions and listen to
what I'm trying to tell you. There is one guest in particular
who'll be wanting to talk to you. His name is Boreal, Lord

Boreal, and he's a spy for the Church, so it is very important indeed that you tell him you're happy in London and that you want to stay. Because the Church is just the tiniest bit cross with me for taking you away from Oxford.

She puts her arms round LYRA.

Yes, it's true. They'd rather you were stuck in that dreary college, where you could be stolen at any moment by . . . well, never mind who by. But I'm not going to let you go, my darling, and I'll tell you the reason.

She looks LYRA *in the eye with great seriousness.*

After the party, after the guests have gone, you and I and dear little Pantalaimon will sit down quietly, and I'll tell you about the work that I want you to do for the General Oblation Board. You're going to be, oh so much more useful to it than any grown-up could be. You'll be meeting other children, less well-off than you, and you'll be giving them the chance to travel.

LYRA. Will I go to the Arctic?

MRS COULTER. If you do well, there will be *lots and lots* of reasons for you to go there. That's something to look forward to, isn't it?

PANTALAIMON *signals 'No'.*

LYRA. Yeah.

MRS COULTER. So that's a promise. Now are you looking your best, I wonder? Up on your feet.

LYRA *stands and* MRS COULTER *inspects her from a distance.*

Not bad. Not bad at all. But not the shoulder-bag, of course. Will you take it off, please?

The GOLDEN MONKEY *paws the shoulder-bag.*

LYRA. Have I got to? I really like it. It's the only thing I've got that belongs to me.

MRS COULTER. But Lyra, it looks absurd to wear a shoulder-bag in one's own home. Take it off!

LYRA. No!

She stamps her foot.

MRS COULTER. I'll ask you one more time. Take off that bag. And never stamp your foot again, either in my sight or out of it.

LYRA. Come on, Pan. Let's go.

She's about to go. The GOLDEN MONKEY *springs on to* PANTALAIMON, *pinning him to the ground.* LYRA *feels pain.*

Stop hurting us! Please!

MRS COULTER (*calm*). I think you'll find that once you remove the bag, he'll let you go.

LYRA *takes off the bag. The* GOLDEN MONKEY *releases* PANTALAIMON.

Thank you. Kiss me.

LYRA *does.*

Now, have the caterers brought enough ice, do you think? Warm drinks are *horrid*.

She goes out. LYRA *holds* PANTALAIMON *close.*

PANTALAIMON. She's evil all through.

LYRA. I hate her!

GUESTS *arrive and the room is full.* LYRA *and* PANTALAIMON *circulate with a tray of canapés.*

MRS COULTER (*calls*). Into the music room, everybody! Hurry!

The GUESTS *move out.* LORD BOREAL *approaches* LYRA.

LORD BOREAL. Good evening, Lyra. Let's give the music room a miss, shall we? I'd greatly enjoy a moment's conversation. I'm Lord Boreal.

LYRA. Yeah, I guessed.

LORD BOREAL. Are you enjoying yourself in London?

LYRA. Sort of.

LORD BOREAL. And is Mrs Coulter keeping you fruitfully occupied? Busy, I mean?

LYRA. Well, up to now it's just been going shopping and having my hair done, stuff like that. But soon, I'm gonna be helping the General Oblation Board.

LORD BOREAL. Are you indeed?

LYRA. Yeah, and I'm going to the Arctic.

LORD BOREAL. So that's where she takes them, is it?

LYRA (*doubtfully*). Yeah, I s'pose it is.

LORD BOREAL. What else have you learned about the General Oblation Board?

LYRA. Well . . . I learned about children, of course. And Dust. And sacrifices. 'Cause that's what an oblate is, that's what I 'eard.

LORD BOREAL. I'm delighted that Mrs Coulter has taken you into her confidence. Though 'sacrifice' is rather a melodramatic way of putting it. The children all come to her willingly, after all.

LYRA *and* PANTALAIMON *recoil in horror, but try to disguise their feelings.*

She was worried, you know, that you might be grabbed off the streets by some over-enthusiastic helper of hers. That was the reason she brought you here. But I knew it would only be a matter of time before she made you a part of her collection team. A child to catch a child . . . and what a charming snippet of bait you'll be! It's surprising, isn't it, that no one has worked it out? 'General Oblation Board'. G.O.B . . . and then . . .

LYRA. . . . the Gobblers. Yes, it's *very* surprising.

LORD BOREAL *goes.*

It's her!

PANTALAIMON. Run for it!

She grabs the alethiometer and they climb out of the window. MRS COULTER *appears in the doorway with the* GOLDEN MONKEY.

MRS COULTER. Lyra? Lyra, what are you doing? Come back at once!

Oxford. Outside the MASTER*'s study. There's a big pile of luggage outside the door. The* MASTER *comes out, carrying another suitcase. He locks the door, turns to go and, to his great alarm, sees* FRA PAVEL.

MASTER. Fra Pavel! I thought you were in Geneva.

FRA PAVEL. What are you doing?

MASTER. I'm going to Scotland. Just for the weekend.

He looks guiltily at the large pile of luggage.

No, the South Coast.

FRA PAVEL. Nonsense. You're running away. Do you really suppose that you can flee the consequences of your actions? Your attempt on Lord Asriel's life was an abject farce. You let the college actually pay for his expedition. You gave Lyra into the hands of Mrs Coulter . . .

MASTER. I thought it was what you wanted!

FRA PAVEL. Did she tell you that?

MASTER. No, not exactly. I was wrong. But . . .

FRA PAVEL. Lyra has run away. The police can't find her and neither can we. Mrs Coulter's Tartar guards are combing the streets to no avail.

MASTER. I know all this, and I can't for the life of me see why everyone is going to such lengths to find a perfectly ordinary girl of twelve.

FRA PAVEL. Ordinary? It has escaped your attention, then, that I have watched her, visited her twice a year ever since she was a baby?

MASTER. I've never known why.

FRA PAVEL. You have an alethiometer here at Jordan College, is that correct?

MASTER. Why do you ask?

FRA PAVEL. The Church has the only other example in the Western world. I'm its official reader. And it has warned me of a prophecy, a witches' prophecy, awesome and strange but true. A child of destiny will be born. The circumstances of Lyra's birth make clear that she is that child.

MASTER. What *is* her destiny?

FRA PAVEL. Lyra will either redeem the Church, will carry it on to greater glory . . . or she will destroy it. Which of the two it will be is a secret that only the witches know. Either way, our future depends on her. And now you know why it's imperative that she's found. Bring me the alethiometer.

MASTER. You mean, the one that belongs to the college?

FRA PAVEL. Obviously. Mine's in Geneva. What you are waiting for? Well?

MASTER. Lyra has it. I gave it to her.

After a moment, FRA PAVEL *attempts a pleasant smile.*

FRA PAVEL. Wait in your study. You will shortly receive a visit.

London. Night and fog. There's a late-night coffee stall. LYRA *and* PANTALAIMON *run on, closely followed by* TARTAR GUARDS. *They hide and the* GUARDS *move on.*

LYRA. Are they gone yet?

PANTALAIMON. Yeah, they went slavering round the corner.

LYRA. Don't cry, Pan. We'll find a place to sleep.

PANTALAIMON. It's all so frightening.

LYRA. Ssh. A nice ham sandwich would warm us up.

PANTALAIMON. Do you think it's safe?

LYRA. It better 'ad be, 'cause I'm starving.

They approach the coffee stall. A MAN *in a top hat and a white silk muffler eyes* LYRA *in predatory fashion.*

STALLHOLDER. Yes, love?

LYRA. Cup of coffee and an 'am sandwich, please.

PANTALAIMON. Don't look round.

TOP-HATTED MAN. You're out late, my dear.

PANTALAIMON. Ignore him.

LYRA. I *am* doing.

STALLHOLDER. Here you are, me love. That'll be two groats.

TOP-HATTED MAN. Allow me.

He pays.

LYRA. Can I have more sugar?

STALLHOLDER. Certainly, love.

The TOP-HATTED MAN *produces a brandy-flask.*

TOP-HATTED MAN. Wouldn't you rather have some brandy in your coffee?

LYRA. No, I don't like brandy.

TOP-HATTED MAN. I'm sure you've never had brandy like this before.

PANTALAIMON. I said, ignore him.

TOP-HATTED MAN. And where are you going to, all alone?

LYRA. I'm going to meet my father.

TOP-HATTED MAN. Oh, your father? Is he someone very important?

LYRA. Yes, he's a murderer.

TOP-HATTED MAN. A what?

LYRA. A murderer. It's his job. He's doing a murder tonight. I got his soap and a clean towel in here, 'cause he's usually all covered in blood when he's finished. There he is now. He looks a bit angry.

The TOP-HATTED MAN *backs away and disappears.*

PANTALAIMON. Lyra the liar!

LYRA. Got rid of him, though, didn' I?

PANTALAIMON. *Now* where're we going?

LYRA. Dunno. We'll find a derelict house or summat.

A security-light flashes on and a siren blows. Two TARTARS *appear with* WOLF DAEMONS. LYRA *and* PANTALAIMON *run and are nearly caught.* TONY COSTA*'s voice is heard:*

TONY. Lyra!

One of the TARTARS *collapses, shot with an arrow. The other is felled by a second arrow.* TONY COSTA *and his fellow-gyptian* BEN *run on, armed with bows and arrows.*

Don't scream! It's me!

LYRA. Who?

TONY. Tony. Tony Costa, Billy's brother. From Oxford, remember? When you threw mud at our boat? And told me some daft tale about a skeleton what done it?

LYRA. Oh Tony, I'm sorry!

TONY. Aye well, never mind about that now. We stumbled across you just in time, and that's what matters. This is my mate Ben, best bow-and-arrow man in the gyptian nation.

BEN. Tartar warriors, those were. Come on, let's not hang about. Our pals'll be waiting for us on board.

LYRA. Where are you going, Tony?

TONY. Well, this is a secret, lass . . .

BEN. Aye, keep it dark. They've got eyes and ears all over the shop, them Gobblers.

TONY. But Lyra here was a mate of Billy's, so it's right that she knows. (*To* LYRA.) Billy and Roger and all the rest of the stolen kids are gonna be rescued.

LYRA. Rescued?

TONY. Aye, there's a ship at harbour, leaving at midnight, under the captaincy of Lord John Faa himself, the Lord of the Western gyptians. And we're sailing it up to the Arctic, to find them kids and to bring 'em back home!

BEN. Look after yourself.

TONY. Aye, stay out of trouble.

They start to go.

LYRA. Oh, Tony, listen . . . I saw a photogram of a man in the snow with his hand held up, like this . . . like he was calling me to the Arctic . . . and Lord Asriel's there, and Roger too, that I swore to rescue. I'm comin' with you!

TONY. Never!

BEN. Forget it!

LYRA. I bloody am!

The interior of a rusty old hulk. JOHN FAA *is there with other* GYPTIANS, *among whom is the aged* FARDER CORAM. LYRA *comes in with* PANTALAIMON.

JOHN FAA. Now where had you got to, gal?

LYRA. I been up on deck, Lord Faa. Pan was trying out being a dolphin, chasing the fish about, wasn't you, Pan?

JOHN FAA. Come on in and sit yourself quietly. Friends, pay heed.

The GYPTIANS *settle and listen.*

You all of you know how we gyptians suffered a lot worse
than most from the Gobblers . . .

1ST GYPTIAN. Except for the foreigner kids and the
homeless kids.

2ND GYPTIAN. Aye, they're crafty, them Gobblers.

JOHN FAA. You're right. They are. And we was stuck for a
way to fight back at 'em, till Tony and Ben here captured a
Gobbler. We don't need to know what they done to 'im, but
he talked all right. Lads, tell 'em.

TONY. He said they take the kids up to the North . . . and
they've got a laboratory there, kind of a hospital thing. And
they . . .

He falters.

BEN. Go on, Tony.

TONY. Well . . . they do experiments on 'em.

1ST GYPTIAN. What kind of experiments?

TONY. He said, like . . . like cutting 'em up.

All are horrified.

2ND GYPTIAN. You mean they kill them?

3RD GYPTIAN. Or torture 'em?

BEN. We don't know. That were the last he said.

JOHN FAA. When I heard that news, I took the advice of
Farder Coram here, who is a seer and a spirit-talker, and as
wise as a tree of owls, and we called on the whole of the
gyptian nation for men and for gold, for to charter this ship
with.

He unrolls a map.

This is where we will shortly arrive. The port of Trollesund,
on the southernmost tip of the land of ice.

2ND GYPTIAN. Is that where the Gobblers are?

JOHN FAA. It's where they land. Their laboratory is further away across the snows, we don't know where. We've got to find that out in Trollesund, along of getting what else we need. Guns, on top of our wretched knives and arrows. Some kind of fighting machine, to match with theirs, and transport, too. Once we're fully equipped, we'll leave this child in a place of safety, and we'll march to the Gobblers' hideout.

There's a chorus of agreement, but:

LYRA. No, that en't right. 'Cause I gotta go there with you.

She continues against a chorus of refusals.

I know all about the Gobblers, 'cause they tried to turn me into one of 'em. Please!

FARDER CORAM. I say . . . let's take her with us.

JOHN FAA. Farder Coram, will you briefly explain your reasoning?

FARDER CORAM. That I will.

All listen.

The roads of chance are long and winding. Them as follows 'em oft-times lose their way . . .

JOHN FAA. Briefly, briefly!

FARDER CORAM. It's all to the point, but I'll jump to the nub of it. When I was in Oxford, Lyra, I heard that the Master give you an object that can help us on our journey. May I see it? Look in my eyes, and see if you trust me.

LYRA *takes out the alethiometer and shows it to him.*

Three little wheels, a circle of pictures and a compass-needle. It's an alethiometer all right. I seen one in China-land many years back. Do you know how to ask it questions?

LYRA. Sort of.

FARDER CORAM. And can you sort of read the answers?

LYRA. No, not really . . .

JOHN FAA. Farder Coram, with all due deference to your age
and wisdom, if she can't work this thing, then it's no more
use to us than a busted alarm clock.

FARDER CORAM. I say we give her a chance. Lyra?

LYRA. All right. I'll ask it if I'm really safe from Mrs Coulter
. . . or if she'll find me.

The MEN *watch sceptically as she sets the needles.*

The Madonna for her, and the baby for me, and this dragon
thing, 'cause that means searching . . . well, it's one of the
meanings.

She holds it in front of her like a microphone.

'Will Mrs Coulter find me?'

She looks at the dial. The GYPTIANS *get impatient.*

JOHN FAA. Well?

LYRA. I'm trying! (*Louder.*) 'Will Mrs Coulter find me? Will
she . . . '

FARDER CORAM. Lyra, if you yell at it like a drunken
donkey-driver, it'll tell you nothing. It's got feelings, just
like we have. Sit yourself easy. Let your mind go free . . .
halfway between sleeping and waking . . . like being a
needle floating on a glass of water. And when the answer
comes, reach down . . . and further down, till you find the
level.

LYRA *relaxes.*

LYRA. It's moving! Yeah . . . The thunderbolt . . . twice at the
baby . . . and a serpent an' a thing like a lizard with big pop
eyes . . . and three times at the elephant. I got it! She's
sending . . . a thing to find me . . . up in the air, I think . . .
yes, flyin', flyin' an' spyin', nasty, angry, lock it up fast . . .
and arrivin' soon. No, now. Right now. It's here.

The GYPTIANS *look round.*

1ST GYPTIAN. I can't see it.

2ND GYPTIAN. Nor me.

3RD GYPTIAN. Still waiting.

JOHN FAA. Back to business. Lyra, go and play over there.

Suddenly, a tiny whizzing object flies into view. The
GYPTIANS scatter. BEN traps it in a beer glass, where it
rattles around, trying to escape.

BEN. I got it! I got it!

JOHN FAA. What in the devil's name is it?

FARDER CORAM. It's a spy-fly, John, sent snooping after us
   by the Gobbler woman. Get it in your smoke-leaf tin. Be
   careful!

Someone does and he manoeuvres the SPY-FLY into it.

   It's built of clockwork that won't never run out, and pinned
   to the spring, there's a bad spirit with a spell through its
   heart. This thing's so monstrous angry at being cooped up,
   that if it ever got out, it'd tear and rip and slash the first
   creature it come across. And Lyra warned us!

LYRA. What did I tell you? I can read it!

4TH GYPTIAN. Land ahoy!

Trollesund. Unfriendly TROLLESUNDERS watch as the
GYPTIANS arrive.

JOHN FAA. We better get out by nightfall. Tony and Ben, you
   go into town. Ask whoever will talk to you, have they seen
   any kids and where did the Gobblers take 'em. Jake and
   Barnaby, look around town for all the firearms you can lay
   your hands on. Farder Coram, you take Lyra back to the
   ship for safety. (*To* LYRA.) Don't move one step from
   there. The rest of you, help me look to our transportation.

All go but LYRA and FARDER CORAM.

FARDER CORAM. I'm off into town meself. I've got a
   message to send to a notable witch from around these parts.

LYRA. A *witch*?

FARDER CORAM. Oh aye, and a powerful one, who just
might lend us a hand. You do exactly as Lord Faa told you,
you hear me?

He goes.

LYRA. Come on.

She and PANTALAIMON *move on.*

PANTALAIMON. What're we doing?

LYRA. We're gonna be helpful.

PANTALAIMON. Like finding kids?

LYRA. Yeah, kids'd be good. Or clues. Or Gobblers, even.
Or . . .

She sees something.

PANTALAIMON. What?

LYRA. I can't *believe* it!

PANTALAIMON. *What?*

LYRA. You remember what Mrs Coulter said was the bravest
fighter on earth? Well, look what we found!

IOREK BYRNISON *comes into view. He's breaking up a
big iron buoy.*

PANTALAIMON. An armoured bear!

LYRA. That's right. He can fight for *us*.

PANTALAIMON. He hasn't got no armour.

LYRA. He must have taken it off to work.

PANTALAIMON. He looks a wreck.

A BEAR-KEEPER *appears with a bottle of spirits, which
he nervously pushes towards* IOREK *with a stick.* IOREK
drinks from the bottle.

Uh-oh. He's a drunk as well.

LYRA. He's still an armoured bear, though, isn't he? Let's go and get him.

She moves forward.

PANTALAIMON. *Get* him? What're you talking about? He'll bite your head off!

LYRA *approaches* IOREK. PANTALAIMON *follows fearfully.* IOREK *glares at* LYRA.

Not so close!

LYRA *moves deliberately to within* IOREK'*s reach.*

IOREK. Who are you?

LYRA. I'm Lyra Belacqua and I got a job to offer you.

IOREK. I've got a job.

LYRA. This is a better one. An' I can pay you. I got three gold dollars.

IOREK. I don't need gold. I need meat and spirits, and these people pay me plenty of both.

LYRA. Yes, I can see that. You've got empty bottles all round you. You even *smell* of drink. Haven't you got any self-respect?

IOREK. None.

PANTALAIMON. Let's go.

LYRA. Shuddup! (*To* IOREK.) Don't you even want to know what I want you to do? It's fighting. It's fighting the people who come to Trollesund with their stolen kids.

IOREK. I've seen those people. They're called the child-cutters. I hate them. But I can't fight them for you.

LYRA. Why?

IOREK. Because I can't fight anyone.

LYRA. Why?

IOREK *roars in desperation.*

IOREK. Because I've got no armour!

LYRA. There's all this metal lying around. Why don't you make some armour out of that?

IOREK. It's useless to me. I made my armour out of iron that fell from the skies in a trail of flame. Without it, I am nothing. I cannot go to war, and war is the sea I swim in and the air I breathe. My armour is my soul, just like your daemon is your soul. And it's been taken from me.

LYRA. Who by?

IOREK. The humans of this town. They gave me spirits to drink until I fell asleep, and then they took my armour away from me. I tried to find it, but I couldn't, so I went mad with rage. Now I must work in this yard until I have paid for the buildings I broke and the people I killed.

LYRA *takes out the alethiometer.*

LYRA. I've got a machine that can answer questions. If I can find out where they've hidden your armour . . .

IOREK. Then I'll fight your enemies and I'll serve you until I die. And I'll never drink spirits again.

LYRA. But you mustn't hurt anyone if I ask you not to. Do you promise me on your honour?

IOREK. On my honour.

LYRA. All right, I'll ask.

She sets and reads the alethiometer.

It's in the house of the priest.

IOREK *raises himself up and roars in frustration.*

IOREK. I want to get it now!

LYRA. Why don't you?

IOREK. Because I promised to work till sunset!

LYRA. If you're as small as me, it's sunset now. Look.

IOREK *crouches to her height.*

IOREK. You're right.

He roars and bounds away.

LYRA. We've got him!

The GYPTIANS *appear, with* FARDER CORAM *and* JOHN FAA *among them.*

BEN. This town is evil! Evil!

2ND GYPTIAN. Let's just get out!

GYPTIANS. Aye! Out!

1ST GYPTIAN. We asked the priest, had he seen any kids, and he set his bloody dogs on us!

He shows a rip in his trousers.

3RD GYPTIAN. You brung us to hell, Lord Faa, where there en't no hope of travelling further on!

2ND GYPTIAN. Aye, where're we goin'? Where? Where?

FARDER CORAM. Friends, listen to me!

They fall silent and listen.

When the present is dark and the future is yet unknown, it is the long-betided past which . . .

The GYPTIANS *groan in frustration.*

All right, I'll jump to the practical bit. I sent a message, friends, to Serafina Pekkala, the Queen of the Lapland witches, and a long-lost friend of my youth-time days. She's sent us a creature to guide us, and here he is.

He calls upwards.

Kaisa!

KAISA, *a snow-goose, appears and lands.*

KAISA. Farder Coram! It's lucky you called. I wouldn't have recognised you in a month of Sundays.

The GYPTIANS *stare at her in alarm.*

2ND GYPTIAN. It's a daemon!

3RD GYPTIAN. But there en't no human attached!

FARDER CORAM. Friends, have no fear! This kind and
intelligent snow-goose is Serafina Pekkala's very own
daemon. For witches, you see, can send their daemons
a whole sight further than what we can. Tell me, Kaisa,
is your mistress still young and beautiful?

KAISA. She is, and she remembers you as handsome as ever
you were.

A knowing sigh of 'Ahs' arises from the GYPTIANS.

FARDER CORAM. Well, it was a long time ago. (*To* KAISA.)
Does she know where the children are?

KAISA. Indeed she does, and I've been sent to guide you!

JOHN FAA. What kind of a place have the Gobblers taken
them to?

KAISA. It's the worst of places. We don't know what they do
there, but there's hatred and fear for miles around. Even the
little lemmings and foxes keep their distance. That's why it
is called 'Bolvangar'. 'Fields of evil.'

LYRA. Is a boy called Roger there?

KAISA. Who is this child?

LYRA. I'm Lyra Belacqua.

KAISA. Lyra Belacqua? My queen will be mightily interested
to know you've come.

LYRA. Why?

KAISA. Because of Lord Asriel, and his plan to travel between
the worlds.

LYRA. Like to the city in the Northern Lights?

KAISA. That world is one, but there are many . . . many . . .
others. They are not in our universe, but they're here, right
next to us, close as a heartbeat, linked with the world we
know. I spread my wings . . .

He spreads his wings.

. . . and brush ten million other worlds, and they know nothing of it. Tell me, Lyra . . .

The BEAR-KEEPER *appears, followed by the* MAYOR *and angry* TOWNSPEOPLE.

BEAR-KEEPER. That's the girl, your worship! She was whispering to the bear, and he went rampaging off!

MAYOR. Gyptians! Gyptians! Always the same!

JOHN FAA. What's goin' on?

LYRA. I found a bear, and he's gonna come with us, that's what.

The GYPTIANS *are alarmed.*

GYPTIANS. A bear?

JOHN FAA. Lyra, what in the name of all that's wonderful made you think we wanted a bear?

MAYOR *(to* JOHN FAA*).* Oh, you know nothing about it, I suppose?

He continues, while the TOWNSPEOPLE *chip in with insults and the* GYPTIANS *answer with abuse.*

That bear is ours! You've got no right to him, none. It's not two weeks since he went roaring drunken around the town, tore down the bank and the police station too, not to mention three innocent citizens lying dead as a doornail in the street!

JOHN FAA. Oh Lyra, Lyra!

LYRA. They'd stolen his armour! It's only natural that he got a bit annoyed. Please let's take him! He'll be a wonderful fighter. He's fierce, he's strong.

JOHN FAA. Lyra, he's as likely to kill us as he is the Gobblers.

LYRA. He's not! He won't hurt anyone if I ask him not to. He's given me his word of honour.

JOHN FAA. Honour? That's a human thing. What's a bear
know about honour?

LYRA. I looked in his eyes and I trusted him. I could see it,
Lord Faa.

*There is a loud crash of a wooden house being knocked
down. The* PRIEST *rushes into view.* IOREK *appears in his
rusty armour. Everyone scatters.* IOREK *chases the* MAYOR,
and is about to knock his head off, when:

No, Iorek! Don't do it!

IOREK *puts down the* MAYOR *and backs away.*

MAYOR. Put this beast in chains!

LYRA. Don't you bloody dare!

MEN *advance with chains. A shot rings out and a* MAN's
hat flies off.

MAYOR. Who did that?

LEE SCORESBY *appears with his rifle. His daemon is*
HESTER, *a hare.*

HESTER. We did. Back off.

JOHN FAA. Who are you?

LEE SCORESBY. Scoresby's the name, Texan by birth, sharp-
shooter by profession, temporarily stranded here with my
balloon-for-hire and a cargo of rifles, owing to a certain
local prospecting outfit that never paid my fee.

He flashes the MAYOR *a dirty look.*

HESTER. Howdy, Iorek.

IOREK. Hello, Hester. Hello Lee!

LEE *and* IOREK *embrace.*

JOHN FAA. Do you know this bear?

LEE SCORESBY. Sure do. Iorek Byrnison an' me fought in
the Tungusk campaign together. He's an awkward critter,

and he ain't exactly looking his best right now, but give him a wash and a brush-up, and he'll be the greatest fighter that you ever saw.

JOHN FAA. So what would you think to him joining our rescue expedition?

LEE SCORESBY. Take me too and I might consider it.

HESTER. Not so fast. What'll you pay?

JOHN FAA. One hundred dollars for the two of you.

HESTER (*outraged*). One hundred dollars! That's ridiculous!

LEE SCORESBY. Done.

He shakes JOHN FAA*'s hand. Applause.* JOHN FAA *addresses the* GYPTIANS.

JOHN FAA. Friends! We're fit and set and ready to go.

He raises his hammer.

Let's march!

GYPTIANS. Aye! To the rescue! To Bolvangar!

LYRA *and the* GYPTIANS *set off through the Northern snows.* IOREK *pounds alongside them and* KAISA *flies ahead, as guide. After a while:*

JOHN FAA. Halt! We're close enough. Here's where we'll stop for the night.

GYPTIANS *point upwards and call.*

GYPTIANS. Look out! Spy-fly!

KAISA. Have no fear! I'll head it off, and meet you all at our destination. Farewell!

The GYPTIANS *bid him farewell as he flies out of sight.*

JOHN FAA. Get some sleep now, boys. We got a big day tomorrow.

They all settle down for the night.

BEN (*to* LYRA). Stay here, gal. I'll get you something warm to keep the chill out.

He goes to get her a blanket. JOHN FAA *approaches.*

JOHN FAA. I've been thinking, Lyra, that your symbol-reader thingummy could be useful. First thing in the morning, ask it how many Gobbler-soldiers are there. I'll come and help you.

He goes.

LYRA. *Help!* What a cheek.

PANTALAIMON. Ask it now.

LYRA *consults the alethiometer.*

LYRA. It's saying that there's a Gobbler place quite near, with Tartar warriors. And they're guarding something. It's strange . . . it's like a child, but it isn't a child.

PANTALAIMON. Maybe it's Roger.

LYRA. Yeah! Let's go and look, when they're all asleep.

IOREK *appears carrying a little metal box.*

What's that?

IOREK. Farder Coram asked me to put his smoke-leaf tin into something stronger. Keep it for him.

LYRA *takes it.*

LYRA. It's beautiful.

IOREK. We armoured bears are skilled in working with metal. And I can do more than any bear alive. What is inside this?

LYRA. An angry spirit.

She puts it to her ear.

Very angry. Mrs Coulter sent it after me.

IOREK *is horrified and amazed.*

IOREK. Mrs Coulter? Do you know her?

LYRA. Yes! She's my worst enemy! What's she got to do with you?

IOREK. She is the woman who destroyed me. If it wasn't for her, I would still be the King of Svalbard, home of the armoured bears.

LYRA. What did she do to you?

IOREK. I had a rival, Iofur Raknison, a bear of enormous strength, but vain and treacherous. Mrs Coulter plotted with him against me and I was cast out of Svalbard to wander the Arctic like a vagrant, till I came to Trollesund.

LYRA. Yeah, she's bad enough for that.

IOREK. There's more. Iofur Raknison seized the throne of Svalbard. He pulled down our ancient fortress of ice and built a palace of stone and marble. Then Mrs Coulter promised to get him a daemon – as though he were a human being! Once that thought was planted in his crafty brain, he could never get rid of it. Now he dreams of daemons, talks of daemons, longs for a daemon. Worst of all . . .

LYRA. What?

IOREK. . . . she did all this, not from some foolish desire to improve our lives. She just wanted gaolers.

LYRA. *Gaolers?*

IOREK. Mrs Coulter had an enemy. She wanted him kept a prisoner in the strongest fortress ever known, guarded by the stubbornest creatures on earth. So she brought Lord Asriel to the castle of Svalbard, and they threw him in chains.

LYRA. *Lord Asriel!*

IOREK. Do you know Lord Asriel *too?*

LYRA. Yes, he's my uncle! Iorek, listen! Once we've rescued Roger, and all the kids, we'll go to Svalbard. We'll free Lord Asriel, and we'll win your throne back, and . . .

IOREK. Do you think, if that were possible, that I wouldn't have done it already? Iofur Raknison has an army of five hundred bears, each as mighty as me . . .

LYRA. Then we'll trick him.

   IOREK *laughs and shakes his head*

IOREK. No one can trick a bear.

LYRA. *You* were tricked by the people in Trollesund.

IOREK. I drank spirits. That's a human thing to do. If I'd been true to my bear-like nature, they would never have got the better of me. Bears can see deceit, we see it as plain as arms and legs. It's a gift we were born with. Just as you have a gift. You can read your truth-telling machine, but grown-ups can't. As you are to them, so am I to a human being.

LYRA. So when I'm a grown-up . . . will I not be able to read it?

IOREK. There is a different kind of gift that comes with learning. Bears don't have it.

   He yawns enormously.

I must rest.

   He goes. LYRA *looks at the spy-fly box, puts it away.*

LYRA. Let's go look for Roger.

   They creep quietly away and through the snows.

I know what we gotta do now. Once we've rescued him and the kids, we'll go to Svalbard, and I'll free Lord Asriel. And I'll use the alethiometer to set him free. And then he'll thank me, won't he? He won't be calling me bothersome or disgusting. And he'll . . .

PANTALAIMON. Forget it.

LYRA. Why?

PANTALAIMON. 'Cause you can't trick bears.

LYRA. You can't trick bears as long as they're true to their bear-like nature. But Iofur Rakniwhatsit's trying to be a human being, isn't he? So maybe he's trickable. And maybe . . . Uh-oh.

They've reached a Tartar camp. TARTAR GUARDS *with*
WOLVES *patrol it.*

PANTALAIMON. Tartars.

LYRA. Ssh. This way.

They slip past the GUARDS *and creep on to a seemingly
empty space.*

PANTALAIMON. There's nothing here.

LYRA. Look.

A small figure can be seen a distance away from them.

Roger? Rodge, is it you?

The figure becomes clearer as it turns towards them. It's
BILLY COSTA. *He looks white, drained and half-alive, and
speaks in a feeble whisper.*

BILLY. You seen my Ratter?

LYRA. That ain't Rodge. It's Billy Costa. Billy, what's wrong?

BILLY. Ratter?

PANTALAIMON, *very alarmed, approaches* BILLY *and
searches all around him.*

PANTALAIMON. *He's got no daemon!*

BILLY. I lost my Ratter.

LYRA. Oh Billy! Billy, what happened?

BILLY. Ratter? Ratter?

He collapses. TARTAR GUARDS *appear with their*
WOLVES. *They put a sack over* LYRA's *head and bundle
her away.*

Bolvangar. Searchlights, a high fence, a watchtower. The
TARTAR GUARDS *deliver* LYRA *to a* NURSE. *She has a*
spooky, robotic manner of speech.

NURSE. Welcome to Bolvangar. What is your name?

PANTALAIMON (*very quietly*). Don't tell 'er.

LYRA. It's Lizzie. Lizzie Brooks.

NURSE. Hello, Lizzie. Have you come a long way? That coat
will need a wash. Let's change it.

She starts putting LYRA *into an institutional gown.*

We'll put your shoulder-bag in your very own locker.
What's inside it? Let's see.

She discovers the spy-fly box.

Oh dear. A funny old box.

She finds the alethiometer.

And what's this? A compass? We'll get you something
pretty and soft to play with, like a doll or a nice woolly
bear.

LYRA. I want them back. And I'm keeping that bag as well.

NURSE. All right. Follow me.

She hands them back.

You have arrived in time for recreation.

She leads LYRA *to the recreation area.* GIRLS *are playing*
apathetically with a skipping rope.

PANTALAIMON. I'm too frightened to look. Have they all got
daemons?

LYRA. Yeah, don't worry.

She joins the other girls.

Hello.

LILY. Hello.

LYRA. I'm Lizzie.

LILY. Hello, Lizzie.

LYRA. What's going on?

LILY. Nothing much.

DAISY. It's just boring really. They give us tests, and then they lie us down and they take our temperature.

LYRA. Yeah, it sounds pretty boring.

DAISY. They're always going on about our daemons. Finding out how heavy they are an' all. They got a weighing-machine, and your daemon gets onto it, and then they write things down and take his photo.

LILY. But it's the Dust they're measuring.

DAISY. Yeah, they talk about Dust non-stop.

JESSIE. I en't dusty. I had a shower yesterday.

DAISY. It isn't that kind of dust. It's Special Dust. Every grown-up gets it in the end. That's what *she* says.

JESSIE. The pretty lady.

LILY. Mrs Coulter.

LYRA. Is she here now?

JESSIE. She *wasn't*, but she's coming today to look at a new machine.

The NURSE *appears with the* BOYS. ROGER *is among them.*

NURSE. Hurry along!

DAISY. Here's the boys.

JESSIE. We're not supposed to talk to 'em, but some of us manage!

They laugh.

NURSE. Girls! No smiling!

ROGER *and* LYRA *see each other.*

LYRA. Rodge!

NURSE. No talking to the girls! Play with the ball.

The NURSE *exits.* ROGER *and* LYRA *manoeuvre themselves into contact.*

ROGER. I can't *believe* it! How did you *get* here?

LYRA. I was kidnapped. Are you all right?

ROGER. No, I never been so frightened ever. It weren't so bad when Billy was here. Then last week they Read 'Is Name Out.

LYRA. What'ya mean?

ROGER. They Read Your Name Out, and you gotta go with 'em. There's one boy says that they give you an operation, an' he heard what a nurse was saying. She said to a kid, 'We're not going to kill your daemon or nothing, it's only a cut.' But I en't seen Billy anywhere, not since then. Look out!

The NURSE *returns with another* NURSE.

NURSE. Children, listen carefully. In a few moments we will have a fire drill.

The fire alarm goes.

That is the fire alarm. Go outside to the assembly point and await further instructions. Off you go.

2ND NURSE. Assembly point! Assembly point!

The CHILDREN *follow the* NURSES *off.* LYRA *and* ROGER *hide.*

ROGER. Where we goin'?

LYRA. Where they can't see us.

They reach a building with a large red sign on the door: ENTRY
STRICTLY FORBIDDEN.

LYRA. Listen, Rodge. There's a whole load of gyptians
   coming to rescue us any minute from now.

ROGER. Honest?

LYRA. Yeah! And it en't just gyptians neither. There's an
   armoured bear, an' a man who flies a balloon from Texas
   an' a witch's daemon, only there en't no witch.

   ROGER *is very upset.*

ROGER. Oh Lyra! What an 'orrible trick to play!

   He continues as KAISA *appears and lands.*

   You come all this way, an' then all you can do is make up
   stories! Lyra the liar!

   He sees KAISA.

KAISA. Greetings, Lyra.

LYRA. Greetings to you, Kaisa!

ROGER. It's true!

LYRA. I told you. Where's the gyptians?

KAISA. There's been a small delay.

LYRA. Oh no!

KAISA. It seems the spy-fly had reported their position. The
   better news is that Serafina Pekkala and her band of witches
   are coming to join the battle. May I suggest that this young
   gentleman prepares the children for a rapid escape?

ROGER. That me?

PANTALAIMON. Tell them we're gonna set off the fire
   alarm . . .

KAISA. That's very good thinking, Pantalaimon.

LYRA. Yeah, an' then they all gotta run outside . . . and take
   their coats and boots and stuff or they'll freeze to death.
   Go on.

ROGER *goes.*

KAISA. You must hide. Mrs Coulter's coming over the brow of the hill in a dog-sleigh.

LYRA sees the forbidden door.

LYRA. I'll go in there.

PANTALAIMON *whimpers.*

PANTALAIMON. No, don't!

KAISA. What's the matter, Pantalaimon?

PANTALAIMON. I have a very unpleasant reaction to that door.

Voices are heard.

DR CADE (*off*). She went this way.

DR WEST (*off*). Yes, here are her footprints!

LYRA. I gotta go somewhere!

She opens the door. It swings open, revealing a cage filled with severed daemons, pressing their faces to the wire and howling. PANTALAIMON leaps into LYRA's arms.

KAISA. Where are the children of these daemons?

LYRA. They've been cut away. That's what they do! They're cutting their daemons away!

PANTALAIMON. Save them! Save them!

KAISA. There is no saving to be done. They're lost for ever. Go!

He flies off. Two DOCTORS appear and grab LYRA.

DR WEST. This is the girl!

DR CADE. What's going on here?

He closes the door.

DR WEST. What have you seen? What have you seen?

LYRA. Leave me alone!

PANTALAIMON. Let her go!

DR CADE. We can't let her go back to the other children. She'll blurt it all out, and we'll have total panic all round.

DR WEST. There's only one thing we *can* do, it seems to me.

DR CADE. What, now?

DR WEST. Why not?

DR CADE. But Mrs Coulter hasn't arrived. I thought she had to be there for each experiment.

DR WEST. That's what she *says* . . . but there's no scientific justification for it. She simply enjoys watching.

DR CADE. Then we just won't tell her. The shock will certainly prevent the girl from talking. Where's Doctor Sargent?

DR WEST. In the laboratory.

They enter a laboratory. DR SARGENT *is there. There's a machine with an operating-chair and a small cage, and a guillotine-blade between the two.* LYRA *is thrown onto the chair.* DR WEST *puts on plastic gloves.*

DR SARGENT. Gentlemen, what very good timing. May we position the subject?

PANTALAIMON. What are you doing?!

DR SARGENT. It's just this moment that I've brought the apparatus up to the testing stage. Now the daemon, please.

DR WEST *grabs* PANTALAIMON *and puts him in the cage. The parting is agonising for both him and* LYRA. *She screams:*

LYRA. You can't touch him! You can't touch him!

DR SARGENT. Reveal the daemon-bond, Doctor West.

DR WEST. Coming right up!

The bond between LYRA *and* PANTALAIMON *is made visible.*

DR SARGENT. Doctor Cade, are you standing by with the resuscitation equipment?

DR CADE. I am.

PANTALAIMON. Lyra! Lyra!

LYRA. Pan!

DR SARGENT (*to* LYRA). Keep still for a moment for me, if you would. That's perfect.

The blade is about to fall. MRS COULTER *appears.*

MRS COULTER. Stop!

She recognises LYRA.

Lyra! Let that child out this instant!

The DOCTORS *release* LYRA *and* PANTALAIMON.

DR SARGENT. But Mrs Coulter . . .

MRS COULTER. No experiments may take place when I am not in attendance. I must see each one.

DR SARGENT. But . . .

MRS COULTER. Each one! Now get out! Get out!

The DOCTORS *go.* MRS COULTER *embraces* LYRA, *who is crying.*

Oh Lyra, Lyra. Poor, poor child. It's all right now. Don't cry.

LYRA. Oh Pan!

She embraces PANTALAIMON.

MRS COULTER. What trouble you've caused. I was beside myself. I've never been so upset. I searched for you all through London.

LYRA. You sent the Tartars after me, and the spy-flies too.

MRS COULTER. I had to, darling. Once I knew you were with those ruffian gyptians . . . and a fine job they made of looking after you. Just think what would have happened if I had arrived a moment later.

LYRA. Why do you do it? How can you be so cruel?

MRS COULTER. Lyra, Lyra, it may *seem* cruel. But it's for scientific progress . . . and the betterment of humanity . . . and yes, for the child's own good. Just one little cut, and then it's safe from Dust for ever after.

LYRA. What's wrong with Dust?

MRS COULTER. Why, everything's wrong, my dearest. Dust is evil and wicked. It doesn't collect around sweet and innocent children . . . but just a little bit later, at what we call the age of puberty? When your daemon settles? Then Dust clusters around you, radiates to and from you . . . and the innocent child begins to have all sorts of nasty thoughts and feelings. And all it takes to stop them happening, is a snip. A tiny snip. The daemon isn't killed. It's simply not connected. It's like a sweet little pet.

LYRA. If cutting's so good, then why did you stop them doing it to me? You should have been glad!

MRS COULTER. Darling, these are grown-up thoughts.

LYRA. They're not! There isn't a kid in the whole world that wouldn't ask you exactly the same thing. 'Cause you'd have done it to Roger, and he's my friend. And you did it to Billy Costa, and I saw him, he's no more'n a ghost!

MRS COULTER. But Lyra, you aren't Billy or Roger. You're . . . you're . . .

LYRA. What?

MRS COULTER *looks at her thoughtfully.*

MRS COULTER. What did they tell you at Jordan College, about where you came from?

LYRA. Came from?

MRS COULTER. I'm asking about your mother and father.

LYRA. They said they was killed in an airship accident.

MRS COULTER. *Were* killed. Except they weren't. Your father was . . . and is . . . a remarkable man. He . . .

LYRA. You mean he's alive?

MRS COULTER. He is. He's . . . Well, I suppose you have to find out some day. He's Lord Asriel.

LYRA. What?

MRS COULTER. You didn't know?

LYRA. No! Lord Asriel? He's my dad? That's *incredible*. And he escaped the airship accident? Yeah, he would. He's ever so clever. But . . . you put him in prison!

MRS COULTER. Lyra . . . !

LYRA. You put my father into a stinky dungeon!

MRS COULTER. I had no choice. Let me finish my story before you condemn and reject me.

LYRA. Well?

MRS COULTER. The airship accident never happened. It was just a story that Lord Asriel invented to deny the facts of the matter. He loved your mother and she loved him. It was a wonderful love. But she was married already. And when you were born, her husband guessed the truth, and Lord Asriel fought him and killed him. No one ever denied that the fight was a fair one, not even at the trial.

LYRA. The *trial*?

MRS COULTER. There was a trial for murder. And the end of it was that Lord Asriel had to give up his estates, his palaces, his enormous wealth . . . though your mother, of course, knew nothing about this. She was so distressed by all that had happened that . . . that she wasn't even able to look after you. And that's when Lord Asriel did something very wrong and cruel. He put you into the care of Jordan

College, and he told the Master that your mother should never be allowed to have anything to do with you. She was banned and shunned from being with her very own daughter. And that's how things stayed until she came to Jordan College and spoke to the Master . . .

LYRA. You mean that . . . ?

MRS COULTER. Yes.

LYRA. You can't be.

MRS COULTER. I am. I'm your mother. Do you understand now why I put your father in prison? It was my only chance to be with you, to hug you and love you, to talk to you frankly as woman to woman. But you're exhausted, poor child. I'll put you to bed. Oh yes. There's just one tiny thing that I have to ask you. The Master told me . . . before his tragic accident . . . that he gave you a certain toy.

LYRA freezes.

It's called an alethiometer. Shall I look after it for you?

After a moment's thought, LYRA *takes out the spy-fly tin and hands it to* MRS COULTER.

Oh, you're keeping it safe in here. Thank you. It's a beautiful little tin . . . not easy to open, though.

She finds a scalpel. The GOLDEN MONKEY *watches as she cuts.*

I'm longing to see what it looks like. Here we are.

With a furious buzz, the spy-fly shoots out and crashes into the GOLDEN MONKEY*'s face.* MRS COULTER *is injured by proxy. Crashes and explosions are heard.* ROGER *rushes into view.*

ROGER. Lyra! Come on! The kids are waiting!

LYRA sets off the fire alarm, and she, ROGER *and* PANTALAIMON *run out . . .*

. . . into the snow. CHILDREN *are there, waving excitedly as the* GYPTIANS *approach.* TARTAR GUARDS, DOCTORS *and* NURSES *appear and attack the* GYPTIANS. IOREK *drives off* TARTAR GUARDS, *and* LEE *fires at individuals with deadly aim. The* GYPTIANS *rescue the* CHILDREN. ROGER *points to the skies.*

ROGER. Look!

SERAFINA PEKKALA *appears on the roof.*

SERAFINA. Lyra Belacqua!

LYRA. Who are you?

SERAFINA. I'm Serafina Pekkala! Seize my hand! We're flying to Svalbard!

LYRA *grabs* SERAFINA *with one hand and* ROGER *with the other.* MRS COULTER *appears with her* GOLDEN MONKEY. *Both are wounded in the same place.* MRS COULTER *extends her arms upwards.*

MRS COULTER. Lyra!

End of Act One.

ACT TWO

Oxford / Oxford. The Botanic Gardens. Night. WILL *and*
LYRA *as before.*

WILL. So . . . while you were ballooning over the icebergs,
I was standing . . . trying very hard not to be noticed . . .
at a bus shelter in Oxford. It was midnight and I'd killed
a man. I'd actually killed him. I'd heard the thwack of his
head as it hit the floor. And I'd run, I'd pelted down the
stairs and legged it into the night. With this. This green
leather case that started it all.

LYRA. What I understand much better now, is how many
different forces were moving us on.

WILL. I knew the coppers'd be after me. By the morning there
wouldn't be a single police car buzzing past that didn't have
my name and photo.

LYRA. There was what I wanted. And there was what you
wanted. And there was what the grown-ups wanted, which
was mostly completely different. But there was also . . .
something bigger than all of us put together . . .

WILL. I didn't know what they did to twelve-year-old
murderers, but it wouldn't be nice . . .

LYRA. . . . like an enormous wind, sweeping us forwards . . .

WILL. . . . and while I was standing . . . shaking with fear . . .
I saw a window in the air. We saw so many of 'em after
that, but this first time is the one I remember best. I looked,
and there was Cittàgazze.

LYRA. . . . taking us to places we didn't even know existed.

WILL. There were little waterside shops and cafés and the
smell of the sea and a warm wind . . .

LYRA. Our fate . . .

WILL. . . . and palm trees.

LYRA. . . . our destiny.

WILL. So I went through.

In the basket of LEE SCORESBY*'s balloon.* SERAFINA
PEKKALA, *on her branch of cloud-pine, tows the balloon.*
LYRA, IOREK *and* ROGER *are out of sight, asleep in the
basket.*

SERAFINA. Are the children asleep down there?

LEE SCORESBY. They sure are, and Iorek too. It looks like
they won't wake up till we get there.

SERAFINA. It won't be long now. See that black line ahead of
us? That's the Svalbard cliffs. We'll have to keep our height
as we fly over them, or the cliff-ghasts will be swooping up
after us all, and me in particular. They've a great liking for
witch-flesh.

LEE SCORESBY. Can't you make yourself invisible?

SERAFINA. I can empty my head of thought so that a short-
lived mortal won't *notice* me. That's not invisible, quite, and
it wouldn't prevail against cliff-ghasts. They have no human
sensitivities for me to cancel out, just hates and appetites.
And what will you do, Mr Scoresby, once we've landed?

LEE SCORESBY. I'll set down Iorek and the kids, and I'll find
a wind to blow me back to Trollesund. Landing Iorek in the
other bear's kingdom could count as an act of war. And like
I told that critter, one bear against five hundred isn't a war.
It's plain suicide.

SERAFINA. But Iorek has sworn to stay with Lyra until he
dies, and that he will do.

LEE SCORESBY. She's pretty important, yeah?

SERAFINA. Are you sure she's asleep?

LEE SCORESBY. Sure is.

SERAFINA. Then I can tell you that she's more important than you can imagine. We witches fly where the veils between the worlds are thin. We hear the whispers of the immortal beings who pass from one to the other. And it's from those whispers that we've knitted ourselves a prophecy. It's in our poems, our spells, the bedtime songs that we sing to our children. It tells of a child of destiny. A child who has it in her power to bring about the annihilation of death and the triumph of Dust.

LEE SCORESBY. Are you saying that Dust is real?

SERAFINA. I know it's real.

She shows him what seems to be a large homemade telescope.

There was a traveller called Jopari, who came from a different world. He gave me this, my amber spyglass. See for yourself.

She hands it to him and he looks through it.

LEE SCORESBY. I can't believe this. What am I looking at?

SERAFINA. It's Dust, Mr Scoresby. Breathing and thinking and flowing to where it will. That is what makes our world a living place. And that's why we witches must keep Lyra safe and sound until the prophecy's run its course.

LEE SCORESBY. So the future's fixed? She's like some clockwork doll, that you wind up and set on a path that can't be changed? Where's her free will?

SERAFINA. We are all subject to the fates. But we must act as though we are not, or die of despair. And Lyra, most of all, must think her fate is malleable. If she tries to follow the prophecy blindly, she will fail. But if she acts in ignorance, out of her own true impulse, then she . . .

PANTALAIMON appears from out of the basket, followed by LYRA, who has been listening.

LEE SCORESBY. She's awake. Hi kid.

LYRA. I was fast asleep. Aren't you freezing, Serafina Pekkala?

The balloon lurches.

What's happening?

SERAFINA. We're flying off course.

LEE SCORESBY. Hell, we're way too high. I'm gonna release some pressure.

He pulls on a rope. Gas escapes from the balloon and it starts rapidly dropping. ROGER *and* IOREK *wake.*

ROGER. Help! Help!

LEE SCORESBY. Nobody panic!

ROGER. I'm gonna be sick!

IOREK. Pull on that rope!

LEE *pulls on another rope to control the descent.*

LEE SCORESBY. That ought to stop it.

LYRA. We're still falling!

SERAFINA. Look out for cliff-ghasts!

LEE SCORESBY. The rope's frozen up. Give us a hammer.

LYRA *helps him pull at the rope.* ROGER *looks for a hammer.*

IOREK. Stand aside! I'll do it.

He goes to the rope. The basket lurches.

ROGER. Please, please! Somebody stop it!

IOREK *pulls at the rope and the basket lurches. A* CLIFF-GHAST *climbs over the edge of the basket.*

IOREK. It's only a cliff-ghast.

He cuffs it and it disappears.

ROGER. Look, there's another!

Another appears. IOREK *lunges at it.* LEE SCORESBY *fires and the basket rocks.*

LYRA. Help!

She lurches over the edge. ROGER *grabs her.*

ROGER. She's fallen out!

LYRA *and* PANTALAIMON *fall out into the snow.* SERAFINA *and* IOREK *call from above.*

SERAFINA. Lyra! I'll come back and find you!

IOREK. Stay away from the fortress! Wait for me!

ROGER. Lyra! Lyra!

On the ground, LYRA *picks herself up.*

LYRA. Pan? Where are you?

PANTALAIMON. In your bag.

He appears out of it as a mouse.

Are you hurt?

LYRA. Dunno.

BEARS *appear. They circle around* LYRA *and sniff her with suspicion.*

CHIEF BEAR. Did you fall out of the balloon?

LYRA. Yeah.

CHIEF BEAR. Was Iorek Byrnison with you?

LYRA. Er . . . Yeah.

CHIEF BEAR. Come wi' us.

They walk on.

STUPID BEAR. Where are we taking her, Sarge?

CHIEF BEAR. To see the King, of course, in his marble palace.

DISGRUNTLED BEAR. 'Marble palace!'

CHIEF BEAR. Now, now, it isn't for us to scoff. That palace were Mrs Coulter's doing, to make us all more civilised-like.

DISGRUNTLED BEAR. 'More civilised-like!'

STUPID BEAR. Mrs Coulter's gonna make it so that we all get daemons, isn't she, Sarge?

CHIEF BEAR. That's what she tells us, so we gotta believe it.

DISGRUNTLED BEAR. Oh, it'll happen all right. Along with all the rest of her fancy notions. Reading and writing and making us cook our food. What I wouldn't give for a mouthful of raw walrus.

The BEARS *slaver with desire at the thought of raw walrus.*

CHIEF BEAR. No grumbling if you please!

They arrive at the palace. Other BEARS *are assembled there.*

(*To the other* BEARS.) Greetings brothers! Find His Majesty, and humbly inform him that we've brought the prisoner.

BEARS *go out.*

LYRA. Are there other prisoners here at Svalbard? Or is it just me?

CHIEF BEAR (*to* LYRA). Do you see that window?

He points to a lit-up window, very high up.

That is Lord Asriel's prison.

He moves away. LYRA *looks up at the window.*

LYRA. It's like a star at the top of the sky. So bright an' far away. An' you just can't get to it.

She takes PANTALAIMON *out of her bag.*

Pan, I've got an idea.

BEAR-COURTIERS *appear with* IOFUR RAKNISON *at the centre. The* BEARS *pay homage to him, while* LYRA *slips* PANTALAIMON *back into her bag.*

BEARS. Hail, King Iofur Raknison!

A BEAR *brings* LYRA *forward to* IOFUR.

IOFUR. You may kneel. Are you a spy?

LYRA. No! No I'm not!

IOFUR. Then what were you doing with Iorek Byrnison?
Don't deny it! You were in the balloon beside him!

LYRA. I'm his daemon.

IOFUR. *His daemon?*

LYRA. Yes.

IOFUR. Clear the court!

The other BEARS *leave.*

If you're deceiving me, you will be fed to the starving
wolves.

LYRA. I know, but I'm not.

IOFUR. How did that renegade outcast get a daemon?

LYRA. It was an experiment at Bolvangar. There was a doctor
pressed a button, and I appeared.

IOFUR. *Liar!* No daemon has ever appeared in a human form!

LYRA. It's 'cause . . . I'm an animal's daemon. Humans have
animals, and animals have humans. It's like, back to front,
all right?

IOFUR. Then how can you travel so far away from him?

LYRA. I'm like a witch's daemon. And beside . . . he's not
very far away. He's coming to Svalbard really soon, and
he's gonna raise up all the bears against you . . . 'cause he's
heard how they grumble about you.

IOFUR *roars.*

Wait, wait, wait . . . And I don't want that to happen, I don't,
'cause he's a poor, sad, drunken disgrace of a bear, and
you're a king with a magnificent palace. So what you gotta

do . . . you gotta tell your guards, that when he arrives . . . they mustn't attack him . . .

IOFUR. Not attack him?

LYRA. . . . an' I'll pretend that I'm still on his side . . . and then you gotta challenge him in single combat! On your own! And when you've beaten him, that'll prove that you're the strongest, and then I'll belong to you! I'll be your daemon! I'll have a little throne of my own, right next to yours, and humans will come from all over the world to wonder at you! King Iofur Raknison, the bear with a daemon!

BEARS *enter in a state of excitement and alarm, as* IOREK *appears in his rusty armour.*

DISGRUNTLED BEAR. Iorek Byrnison is here!

BEARS. Iorek is here! Iorek is here!

STUPID BEAR. Shall we kill him?

IOFUR. Leave him to me. Bring me my armour! I'll kill him myself!

Other BEARS *dress* IOFUR *in armour.* LYRA *runs to* IOREK.

LYRA. Oh, Iorek, I've done a terrible thing. You've got to fight Iofur Raknison all alone, and you're hungry and tired . . .

IOREK. How did this happen?

LYRA. I tricked him! Oh, I'm sorry.

IOREK. You are no longer Lyra Belacqua. Your name for ever after will be Lyra Silvertongue.

LYRA. You mean I haven't done wrong?

IOREK. Done wrong? To fight him is all I want!

IOFUR *addresses the crowd.*

IOFUR. Bears! Hear my command! If I kill Iorek Byrnison, his flesh will be torn apart and scattered to the cliff-ghasts. His head will be stuck on a pole above my palace gates.

His name will be blotted from memory. Iorek Byrnison,
I challenge you!

IOREK *addresses the crowd.*

IOREK. Bears! If I kill Iofur Raknison, I'll be your rightful
king. My first order to you will be to tear down this palace,
this perfumed house of mockery and tinsel, and hurl it into
the sea. Iofur Raknison has polluted Svalbard. I shall
cleanse it.

Trumpets. IOFUR *and* IOREK *square up for the fight. They
prowl round, sizing each other up. They pause. They leap
together with a crash. They fight and* IOREK's *left forepaw
seems to be wounded.* IOFUR *taunts him.*

IOFUR. Whimpering cub! Prepare to die!

IOREK *leaps at him: the injury was only a feint. He tears
off part of* IOFUR's *jaw and sinks his teeth in his throat.*
IOFUR *dies.*

IOREK. Behold! I eat the heart of the usurper!

He tears out IOFUR's *heart and eats it.*

Now who is your king?

BEARS. Iorek Byrnison!

They rush to support IOREK, *who is near collapse.* ROGER
appears.

ROGER. What happened? Have I missed it?

LYRA. Iorek ate the other bear's heart.

ROGER. Eurgh! Yuk!

LYRA. Come on, Rodge, we're going to find Lord Asriel.

She pulls him along through the palace and up stairs.

ROGER. The balloon crashed into a mountain. And then that
goose arrived and said that one of the witches got made a

prisoner at Bolvangar, so Serafina went back to rescue her. She was frightened the witch might tell them something. Then . . .

THOROLD *appears.*

THOROLD. Lyra! Little Lyra! Come in, child, and bring your friend with you. The Master is in his study.

He leads LYRA *and* ROGER *to a door.*

LYRA (*to* ROGER). In his *study*? I thought he was put in chains.

THOROLD. You know the Master. He hadn't been here a month before he'd twisted the bears around his little finger. They gave him books and instruments and a laboratory. He was both prisoner and prince.

LYRA *goes into* LORD ASRIEL's *study.* LORD ASRIEL *is working on a piece of scientific equipment. He looks up and sees her.*

LORD ASRIEL. Lyra! Get out! I did not send for you!

LYRA *is dumbfounded.*

LYRA. What?

ROGER *comes in.*

STELMARIA. She's brought a friend.

LORD ASRIEL. Who's this boy?

LYRA. He's Roger. You saw him at Jordan College.

LORD ASRIEL. Come here, Roger.

ROGER *approaches him.* LORD ASRIEL *looks at him hard. Smiles.*

I'm delighted to see you. Thorold, run these children a hot bath.

ROGER. Wow!

THOROLD. Follow me.

*LORD ASRIEL goes back to his work. THOROLD leads
ROGER out. LYRA stays. LORD ASRIEL looks up and
sees her.*

LORD ASRIEL. I thought you'd gone.

LYRA. I'm not some bloody kid that you can have put in the
bath when you feel like it. You're my father, en't you?

LORD ASRIEL. Yes. So what?

LYRA. So what? You should have told me before, that's what.
You could've asked me to keep it secret, and I would've. I'd
have been so proud that nothing would have torn it out of
me. But you never.

LORD ASRIEL. How did you find out?

LYRA. My mother told me.

LORD ASRIEL. Your mother . . . ? Then there's nothing left
to talk about. I don't intend to apologise, and I refuse to be
preached at by a sanctimonious ten-year-old.

LYRA. I'm twelve! I'm twelve!

LORD ASRIEL. Well, you would know. If you want to stay,
you'd better make yourself interesting to me. Tell me about
your journey here. What have you seen? What have you
done?

LYRA. I set you free, that's what I done. You can go.

LORD ASRIEL. I'll go when I'm ready. What else?

LYRA. I brought you this. The Master give it me.

She shows him the alethiometer.

I hid it and I treasured it and I kept on going, even with
Tartars and Gobblers catching me, and being nearly cut
away from Pantalaimon. And after all that, when I walked
in the door, you looked horrified, like I was the last thing
in the world you wanted to see.

LORD ASRIEL. But Lyra . . . you were.

LYRA. Right, that's it. You're not my father. Fathers love their daughters. But you don't love me, and I love a moth-eaten old bear more than I love you. Here, take it anyway.

She gives him the alethiometer.

LORD ASRIEL. I can't read this thing. It will only annoy me. Keep it.

LYRA. But . . .

LORD ASRIEL. Don't argue with me.

He gives it back to her. She's very upset.

LYRA. So it was all for nothing.

LORD ASRIEL. Nothing? What if I told you that you'd helped me? That in your childish innocence, you'd brought me the key to a door that had never been opened? And that behind that door lay the greatest adventure that the human race has ever known?

LYRA. I dunno what you're talkin' about.

LORD ASRIEL. Well, think. You were at Jordan College. You overheard my lecture. Didn't you understand what I was saying?

LYRA. Yeah, 'course I did! There was Dust, and that Jopari man with his hand held up like that. An' it was him what gave you the amber something? Wasn't it?

LORD ASRIEL. He gave me that and a great deal more.

LYRA. There was the palm trees, and the Roarer . . .

He laughs.

LORD ASRIEL. The Roarer!

LYRA. Don't laugh! I gotta find out these things. What's a . . . nylation?

LORD ASRIEL. A nylation?

LYRA. Yeah. A nylation of death. What's the Triumph of Dust? What if you're just a clockwork doll, but nobody tells you? What's Dust anyway?

LORD ASRIEL. Either you've been eavesdropping more than I suspected, or you've an uncanny imagination. Dust is like a vast, invisible ocean all around us. It thinks for itself, it's conscious. And it settles on adults, never on children. It's the physical proof that something happens when innocence becomes experience.

LYRA. Like how?

LORD ASRIEL. Like Adam and Eve in the Garden of Eden. Do you know what original sin is?

LYRA. Sort of.

LORD ASRIEL. Eve fell, and the human race lost its innocence. It gained experience in return. And for the very first time, Dust entered the world. Dust loves experience. It loves what we learn, what we remember, what we make of ourselves. That's why it terrifies those poor, sad, stunted souls in Geneva. They hate the power that we have when we're truly alive. Your mother made use of that, to get the Church to pay for her experiments.

LYRA. You done experiments too, though. Do you cut children?

LORD ASRIEL. Oh, no. Cutting in itself is merely random cruelty. My experiment draws on something that your mother's bumbling doctors never noticed. You see, when the daemon-bond is severed . . . cut right through . . . it releases a burst of energy. Greater than any earthquake, any bomb ever made. If we could *use* that energy . . .

Pause.

LYRA. We could travel to other worlds.

He smiles approvingly.

LORD ASRIEL. Bravo.

LYRA. There's millions of other worlds, en't there?

LORD ASRIEL. There are as many worlds as there are possibilities. I toss a coin. It comes down heads. But in another world, it comes down tails. Every time that a choice is made, or a chance is missed, or a fork in a road is taken . . . a world is born for each of the other things that *might* have happened. And in those worlds they do. Somewhere out there, in one of those worlds, is the origin of all the death, the sin, the misery, the destructiveness in the world. I'm going to destroy it.

LYRA. You never said nothing about any of this. Not at Jordan.

LORD ASRIEL. Do you really imagine that I'd tell those scholars what I was planning? If the Church suspected, for one moment . . .

STELMARIA. You've told her enough.

LORD ASRIEL. Stelmaria is right. She's always right. Have your bath.

LYRA. Can we talk in the morning? Can I ask you questions?

LORD ASRIEL. Ask me whatever you like. You're my daughter. Now go.

He turns away from her. LYRA *goes.*

Bolvangar, partly destroyed. SERAFINA *is there. She makes herself invisible and watches the action unseen.* MRS COULTER *arrives to find* LORD BOREAL.

MRS COULTER. Lord Boreal? What in the world are you doing at Bolvangar? How did you get here?

LORD BOREAL. I arrived by zeppelin, my dear, with a party of eminent clerics from the Consistorial Court of Discipline. They plan to conduct an interrogation, and I've been asked to help.

MRS COULTER. Are you going to interrogate *me*?

LORD BOREAL. Well, not today. I can't, of course, give any assurance for the future. No, you captured a witch in the course of the recent battle, and Fra Pavel believes that she holds vital information. Here she is.

FRA PAVEL *and other* CLERICS *bring on a* WITCH
bound to a chair. She has been tortured.

MRS COULTER. Let that witch go! You haven't the right to
lay one finger on her. She's the private property of the
General Oblation Board!

FRA PAVEL. There is no General Oblation Board. It's been
closed down and its records have been expunged. Your spy-
flies are decommissioned, and your bank account in Geneva
was terminated at midnight.

MRS COULTER. I can explain what happened.

FRA PAVEL. We know what happened. The Church's entire
investment in Bolvangar has been wiped out. We know that
your daughter was responsible. What we do not know, and
are here to find out, is what her future holds.

MRS COULTER. Forgive me, Fra Pavel, this is much too
subtle for me to understand. Just what are you talking
about?

FRA PAVEL. What do you know about the witches' prophecy?

MRS COULTER. I've never heard of it. What does it say?

FRA PAVEL. It states reliably, most reliably, that Lyra is either
the Church's greatest friend or its darkest foe.

MRS COULTER. Lyra? Lyra my daughter. How long have you
known?

FRA PAVEL. Since she was born.

MRS COULTER. Well, I'll do all that I can to help.

FRA PAVEL. I thought you might. Where is Lyra now?

MRS COULTER. She's . . . ah . . . flown to Svalbard.

FRA PAVEL. Correct.

MRS COULTER. May I go?

LORD BOREAL. No, you may not. Fra Pavel, has this witch
co-operated with your enquiries?

FRA PAVEL. She's told us nothing.

He hits the WITCH.

LORD BOREAL. Perhaps the feminine touch would be more effective. Mrs Coulter, would you be so good as to take over the questioning?

MRS COULTER. Now?

LORD BOREAL. Yes, now. We need her to tell us precisely what this prophecy means. Is Lyra good or evil? Should we celebrate her as our saviour, or must we hunt her down? Proceed.

MRS COULTER *takes the* WITCH*'s hand.*

MRS COULTER. Well, witch! You heard Lord Boreal. What is the answer?

The WITCH *shakes her head.* MRS COULTER *breaks one of her fingers.*

MRS COULTER. *Now* will you tell us?

WITCH. Never!

MRS COULTER. Tell us!

She breaks another finger.

Tell us, or I will break *all* your fingers!

The WITCH *cries.*

WITCH. It's in the name!

FRA PAVEL. The name?

MRS COULTER. What name?

WITCH. Lyra Belacqua has a secret name! All that you want to know is in that name! But you will never find it out!

MRS COULTER (*to* LORD BOREAL). Is there really any purpose in . . .

LORD BOREAL. Don't stop now!

MRS COULTER. What is the name? Tell us!

WITCH. It is the name of one who came before. You've always feared her. Now she has come again!

FRA PAVEL. Lyra's our enemy.

MRS COULTER. That's not what she said.

1ST CLERIC. We must fly to Svalbard.

2ND CLERIC. We must capture and interrogate her.

LORD BOREAL. Not yet. (*To* MRS COULTER.) Continue.

MRS COULTER. Must I?

FRA PAVEL. We need the name!

   MRS COULTER *turns slowly to the* WITCH.

MRS COULTER. Tell us the name. Tell us the name!

   She breaks another finger.

WITCH. Serafina Pekkala! Let me die!

   SERAFINA PEKKALA *becomes visible.*

SERAFINA. I am here.

   She stabs the WITCH.

FRA PAVEL. Seize her!

   SERAFINA *draws her bow and arrow. Pandemonium.*
   SERAFINA *escapes.*

The Palace at Svalbard. Night. The BEARS *are celebrating.*
THOROLD *appears.*

THOROLD. Miss Lyra! Miss Lyra!

LYRA. What's up?

THOROLD. The Master's packed a sledge and gone up North.
   And he's taken the boy.

LYRA. What, taken Roger?

THOROLD. Don't you remember? He said, 'I did not send for
   you.'

LYRA. You mean he'd sent for someone else?

THOROLD. He'd sent for a child to finish his experiment. That's his way. Whatever he wants, he calls, and along it comes.

LYRA. And I walked in . . . and he thought it was me. But he's not gonna do what I *think* he is? He *can't*.

PANTALAIMON. He'll do it for sure. He wants that burst of energy.

LYRA (*calls*). Iorek! We gotta find Lord Asriel! *Now!*

IOREK. Bears! March on to the mountains!

LYRA *and* PANTALAIMON *join the* BEARS *as they all march to the mountains.*

LYRA (*to* IOREK). Faster! Fast as you can!

IOREK. What's that sound?

LYRA. There's a zeppelin coming after us!

FRA PAVEL*'s amplified voice is heard from the zeppelin:*

FRA PAVEL. Lyra Belacqua! We can see you!

PANTALAIMON. Who is it?

LYRA. It's the Church! The Church!

Machine-gun fire is heard.

IOREK. Faster! We'll get ahead of them.

They reach a snow-bridge.

Stop! This bridge is made of snow. It will not carry my weight.

LYRA. I'll go on my own. And if ever we meet again . . .

IOREK. . . . . I'll fight for you as though we'd never been parted. Goodbye, Lyra Silvertongue.

LYRA. Goodbye, King Iorek Byrnison.

He goes.

(*To* PANTALAIMON.) Let's go.

They cross the bridge and reach the mountain-top. The Aurora appears. LORD ASRIEL *is there beside a sledge-cum-laboratory, which includes a cage in which* ROGER's *daemon,* SALCILIA, *is imprisoned.* ROGER *is tied up.* STELMARIA *guards him.* LORD ASRIEL *is preparing a handheld blade. He sees* LYRA.

ROGER. Lyra! He's got my daemon!

LORD ASRIEL. Lyra! Get away! This is nothing to do with you.

LYRA. Don't touch her! Leave her alone!

LORD ASRIEL. If you distract me now, I swear I'll strike you dead.

LYRA. He's my friend! Don't you care about that?

ROGER. Lyra, help!

LORD ASRIEL (*to* LYRA). Stay where you are! Stelmaria!

LYRA *releases* ROGER. PANTALAIMON *attacks* STELMARIA. SALCILIA *is released and scooped up by* ROGER.

ROGER. I've got her! I've got her!

LYRA *dashes towards* ROGER. PANTALAIMON *flies to them. For a moment,* LYRA, PANTALAIMON, ROGER *and* SALCILIA *are all together.*

LYRA. Roger, run!

She and PANTALAIMON *run.* STELMARIA *retrieves* SALCILIA *and scares* ROGER *back so he can't approach her.* LORD ASRIEL *cuts boy and daemon apart. The Aurora dips and flares.* ROGER *rises unsteadily to his feet.*

Roger! Roger, speak to me!

ROGER. Feel funny.

He falls to the ground. Above them, STELMARIA *is holding* SALCILIA *up in triumph.*

LYRA. He's *killed* him!

MRS COULTER *is heard approaching.*

MRS COULTER. Lyra!

PANTALAIMON. Quick, hide!

They do. The GOLDEN MONKEY *bounds into view.* MRS COULTER *follows.*

MRS COULTER. Lyra?

LORD ASRIEL. Look, Stelmaria! Look!

On LORD ASRIEL*'s level, a city appears in the Aurora.*

MRS COULTER. Asriel!

LORD ASRIEL. Look at that pathway! Look at the sun . . . it's the light of another world! Don't turn your back on it, Marisa.

She approaches him.

MRS COULTER. Was Lyra here? Did you cut her? Tell me!

LORD ASRIEL. I cut the boy. And it worked! Look at the Dust that's bathing us both in glory. Feel the wind . . . let it blow on your hair, your skin . . .

Their DAEMONS *move closer together.* LORD ASRIEL *and* MRS COULTER *kiss.*

MRS COULTER. Let me go!

LORD ASRIEL. I'll tell you a secret. Nobody knows but you. I'll go through to that world, then into another, on and on, until I've found the Authority. Then I'll destroy him.

MRS COULTER. You're insane.

LORD ASRIEL. Come with me, Marisa. We'll work together. We'll smash the universe into pieces, and put it together in a new way. Isn't that what you want? To be part of my plan?

MRS COULTER. I can't. I have to stay in this world and find our daughter. She's in danger from the Church.

LORD ASRIEL. And you'll protect her?

He laughs.

You of all people? You lied to her. You tried to corrupt her. You put her father in prison. If I were her, I'd run from you as fast as my legs would take me, and I'd keep on running.

The zeppelin is heard.

VOICE (*from the zeppelin*). Lyra Belacqua! Give yourself up! Walk into an open space and raise your hands.

MRS COULTER. *Now* do you believe me?

LORD ASRIEL. Why do they want her?

MRS COULTER. What have you done to deserve to know? Go to your Dust, your filth.

LORD ASRIEL. Go to your dreary, sad little machinations.

Their DAEMONS move apart.

MRS COULTER (*calls*). Lyra? Lyra, are you here?

She walks away and out of sight.

LORD ASRIEL. I don't need you!

LORD ASRIEL *and* STELMARIA *walk into the Aurora.*

LYRA. What do we do? We can't go back.

PANTALAIMON. We gotta go forward, then. To where the Dust is.

LYRA. I'm frightened, Pan.

PANTALAIMON. Me too. But if your mother, and all those other wicked people think that Dust is bad, it's probably good. And don't you remember what Lord Asriel said?

LYRA. It's 'heads in one world, tails in another . . . '?

PANTALAIMON. Roger's dead in this world . . . but there could be another world where he's still alive. And we promised to find him.

LYRA. Come on.

She and PANTALAIMON *climb up, walk into the Aurora and go through it.*

Lapland. SERAFINA *is addressing an assembly of* WITCHES. *They include* PIPISTRELLE, CAITLIN, GRIMHILD *and* GRENDELLA. LEE SCORESBY *is there.*

SERAFINA. Sisters, listen to me! The prophecy has begun and the child is amongst us. And now the Church is after her!

PIPISTRELLE / WITCHES. Do they know her name?

WITCHES. Ssh! / That name is secret! / Not in front of the stranger!

LEE SCORESBY. Ladies, ladies! I'm here with the honest intention of helping you find this child.

SERAFINA. Have you children of your own, Mr Scoresby?

LEE SCORESBY. No. I never married, I'm childless and . . . well, it seems to me that this little kid had a lousy deal from her true parents, and somebody ought to make it up to her.

SERAFINA. I believe you, and I'll tell you as much as any short-lived mortal is allowed to know. Lyra's secret name contains the whole of her destiny. If the Church were to find it out, they wouldn't just send a zeppelin after her. They'd set all their armies on catching and killing her. That's why we witches have to search for her through the maze of the worlds and keep her safe.

RUTA SKADI. Let me speak!

SERAFINA. Ruta Skadi, Queen of the Latvian witches, let's hear you.

RUTA SKADI. If Lyra Belacqua is truly the child of destiny, then destiny will protect her. It doesn't need us to go chasing after.

SERAFINA. So what do we do?

RUTA SKADI. We fight! Lord Asriel's gone to kill the Authority. That means war, and we witches are in that war already, like it or not, because we *know our enemy*. Who hates everything that's good about human nature? Who hates the touch of flesh that we witches live by? Who cut boys and girls away from their daemons at Bolvangar, so that they'd never know the beauty of love? Who persecutes us, who tortures us? Who burns witches?

WITCHES. The Church!

RUTA SKADI. The Church! We've waited hundreds of years for a chance to attack it, and now that chance has come. Let's take it! Now!

SERAFINA. Ruta Skadi, I hate the Church just as much as any witch here. But if we don't first make the prophecy come true, then there won't be a world for you to fight in. Lord Asriel didn't just build a pathway. He cracked the shell of the sky. Look through my amber spyglass. What do you see?

She passes the amber spyglass to GRENDELLA, *who looks through it.*

GRENDELLA. Dust is flowing away.

There's a general gasp of worry and alarm. GRENDELLA *passes on the amber spyglass and more* WITCHES *look through it.*

SERAFINA. All across the North, raggedy doors and windows have opened that were never there before. Dust is falling through them into a void, an absence, and so it will go on, worse and worse, till nothing is left, not a breath, not a gasp, unless the child of the prophecy, true to her secret name, brings not the defeat of Dust, not the loss of the loveliest gift of the stars, but its joyful return. That's why we must guard and protect her, till the prophecy has run its course.

PIPISTRELLE. How can this short-life help us?

WITCHES. Tell us! / How?

LEE SCORESBY. I've been dreaming about a man who I fought beside one time. He was a soldier from another world. But when I see him in my dream, he's changed, he's like some tribal medicine-man. He knows where Lyra's run away to. And I've seen where he's hiding out, I dreamed it like I was seeing it on a map. I can lead you to him in my balloon. He'll take you to Lyra.

RUTA SKADI. What's his name?

LEE SCORESBY. Jopari.

A sigh of recognition from the WITCHES.

RUTA SKADI. Your dream is true. But I can't follow it.

SERAFINA. Where will you go, while we fly onwards?

RUTA SKADI. I'll fly to the battlefield, to fight for Lord Asriel. When you see Jopari, tell him I've not forgotten that he rejected me. I have an arrow for his heart. If I see him, I'll kill him. Farewell.

Cittàgazze. LYRA *and* PANTALAIMON *come on. They have been walking for days.*

LYRA (*calls*). Hello!

No answer.

There's nobody here either.

PANTALAIMON *bounds off towards a café.*

Hey, where're you goin'?

PANTALAIMON. It's a sandwich.

LYRA *looks at it.*

LYRA. It's days old.

She eats a bit of salami out of the middle.

There's one good thing. We're probably safe from my mother and father.

PANTALAIMON. The two most treacherous, lyingest people on all the earth.

LYRA. Wasn't it awful when they kissed like that?

PANTALAIMON. We made some friends though, didn't we?

LYRA. Yeah . . . Iorek . . . Serafina . . .

PANTALAIMON. . . . Kaisa . . .

LYRA. . . . Mr Scoresby . . .

PANTALAIMON. . . . Hester . . .

A noise is heard in the kitchen at the back of the café.

LYRA. What was that?

PANTALAIMON. Let's go an' look.

LYRA. We could have imagined it.

PANTALAIMON. Yeah.

LYRA. Nah, come on.

They go to the kitchen and go to open the door. WILL charges out and into her. They tussle. Then they pull apart and look at each other.

WILL. You're just a girl.

LYRA. You're just a boy. You wanna make summing of it?

WILL. No! I thought that . . . never mind. What's your name?

LYRA. Lyra Silvertongue.

WILL. I'm Will. Will Parry.

She looks at him in horror.

What you lookin' at?

LYRA. What 'appened?

WILL. What?

LYRA. Did they do it to you as well?

WILL. What you talkin' about?

LYRA. Your daemon! Where's your daemon?

WILL. My *demon*?

LYRA. Yeah. Like Pan.

WILL. I haven't got a demon. I don't *want* a demon. Are you talkin' about that cat?

PANTALAIMON. I think he really doesn't know.

WILL. It talks!

PANTALAIMON. Of course I talk. Did you think I was just a pet?

WILL. That's incredible. A talking cat! Now I've seen everything. Is it . . . Can I pat it?

PANTALAIMON. No!

LYRA. Nobody pats another person's daemon. Never, ever.

WILL. I was trying to be nice, that's all. Where I come from, a demon is something evil, something devilish.

LYRA. Where is it? Where you come from?

WILL. It . . . No, you wouldn't believe it.

LYRA. I might.

WILL. All right. I come from a different world.

LYRA. You too?

WILL. What do you mean, 'you too'?

LYRA. Well . . . So do I.

WILL. Honest?

LYRA. Yeah.

WILL. So . . . how did you get here?

LYRA. Through the Aurora.

WILL. Rubbish!

LYRA. What about you, then?

WILL. I came through a window in the air. Near a bus shelter in Oxford.

LYRA. That's impossible.

WILL. Yeah, and walking through the Aurora, that's just normal, I suppose. Tell you what. I'll pretend to believe you, and you pretend to believe me, and then we won't have to row. All right?

LYRA. Look, I don't mind.

WILL. You hungry?

LYRA. Yeah, a bit.

WILL. There's eggs in there. I'll cook an omelette.

He goes to the fridge.

LYRA. Boys can't cook.

WILL. Well, this boy's had to.

LYRA. In my world, servants do the cooking.

WILL. In my world, the Coke is brown.

He produces a couple of bottles of green Coke. Gives her one.

LYRA. It's cold.

WILL. 'Course it's cold. Haven't you ever heard of a fridge?

He mixes eggs and makes an omelette. Two children, ANGELICA and her younger brother PAOLO, appear.

ANGELICA. Hello.

LYRA. Hello.

WILL. What's the name of this place?

ANGELICA. Cittàgazze.

WILL. Where've all the grown-ups gone?

ANGELICA. They all screamed and ran away. It's nice for kids. We can go anywhere we like, and play on the pedal-boats.

PAOLO. There'll be more kids coming back later.

ANGELICA. We're the first.

PAOLO. Along with Tullio.

ANGELICA. Shut up.

LYRA. Who's Tullio?

ANGELICA. He's our brother, that's all.

PAOLO. He's a grown-up. He's up in the tower. He's gonna . . .

ANGELICA. Shut up, I said.

They start shouting at each other.

WILL. Hold it, hold it . . . What did the grown-ups scream and
run away from?

ANGELICA. The Spectres, of course.

LYRA. The *Spectres*?

ANGELICA. Yeah, they're everywhere. They eat people up
from the inside out.

PAOLO. They suck their souls out!

ANGELICA. But they don't bother kids, and kids can't see
'em.

WILL. You mean, there could be a Spectre right next to us
now?

The KIDS *laugh.*

PAOLO. Not just one!

ANGELICA. There's prob'ly hundreds!

PAOLO. We're looking for ice creams. Wanna come?

LYRA. No, not now.

ANGELICA. Snob.

She and PAOLO *go.*

WILL. Spectres all round us.

LYRA. No wonder the grown-ups ran.

WILL. They ran all right.

LYRA. Left their papers.

WILL. Left their food.

LYRA. Left their smoke-leaf.

WILL. Ciggies.

LYRA / WILL. What?

They look at a packet of cigarettes.

Is that what you call 'em?

Pause. They look at each other and begin to believe each other's story.

LYRA. That's funny.

WILL. Yeah. So what're you doing here?

LYRA. I'm looking for someone. And I'm running away as well.

WILL. Who from?

LYRA. My mother, mostly.

WILL. Fed up with you, is she?

LYRA. Worse than that, 'cause I let a spy-fly loose an' I wrecked her laboratory, and I found out the Gobblers' secrets and I'm summing to do with Dust. Special Dust. Not ordinary dust, obviously.

WILL. No, obviously.

PANTALAIMON. What about you?

WILL. I'm running away as well.

PANTALAIMON. Who from?

WILL. Some people.

PANTALAIMON. Bad people?

WILL. Some of 'em are. (*To* LYRA.) Who do I talk to? You or it?

LYRA. It's 'him'. And it makes no difference. If you talk to Pan, you're talking to me in a different way.

WILL. Like on the telephone?

LYRA. What's a telephone?

WILL. Don't you know anything?

LYRA. I do! I know lots of things, but I don't know anything about your world 'cause I've never been there! That good enough for you?

She cries.

WILL. I'm sorry.

LYRA. It en't you. It's just everything that's been happening.

WILL. I do believe you now. I'm starting to.

LYRA. Me too.

WILL. Let's eat.

They eat.

LYRA. Except it can't be true about the window.

WILL. Well, how do you think I got here? I saw the palm trees and the . . .

LYRA. Yes, I believe the window an' the palm trees. But it can't have been in Oxford. I oughta know. I come from Oxford. Oxford's in *my* world.

WILL. Then there's two different places with the same name.

LYRA. Are there scholars in that Oxford?

WILL. Sure are.

LYRA. Is there a Jordan College?

WILL. No, I don't think so.

LYRA. So it's the same but different. Two Oxfords. In two different worlds.

WILL. Two?

LYRA. There could be more. There could be millions. 'I spread
my wings, and brush ten million other worlds, and they
know nothing of it.'

WILL. Who said that?

LYRA. A witch's daemon.

WILL. Right.

LYRA. A snow-goose.

WILL. Right, right.

LYRA. You bet it's right.

WILL. So . . . are you gonna go back? To your dusty world?

LYRA. I can't, not ever. Are you gonna go back to your
different Oxford?

WILL. Uh huh.

LYRA. What's that mean?

WILL. Means I've got to, 'cause I'm looking for someone.

LYRA. Will. Remember I said I was looking for someone too?
Well, him an' me was best friends, and he used to live in *my*
Oxford.

WILL. So?

LYRA. Can I come with you?

WILL. Yes, if you want. Just don't come trailing around after
me, that's all. You'll need some proper clothes. We'll have
to borrow 'em from a shop.

LYRA. What's wrong with what I got on?

WILL. My world is dangerous for me. Really dangerous. An'
if people notice us, they're gonna start wondering where we
come from, and then they'll find the window and I won't
have this world to come an' hide in. So you gotta fit in. And
don't talk to anyone. Got that?

LYRA. Yeah.

WILL. And wash your hair. And have a bath. If you go round smelling like that, you're really gonna stand out.

He gets up.

I cooked, so you can wash up.

LYRA. I don't wash up.

WILL. Then I won't show you the window. This place doesn't belong to us. So we gotta tidy up after ourselves. I'll find a bed upstairs. Good night.

He takes the leather writing-case and goes.

LYRA. That's the grumpiest boy I ever met.

PANTALAIMON. Find out who he is.

LYRA. I will.

She takes out the alethiometer and studies it.

PANTALAIMON. What's it say?

LYRA. It says he's a murderer. He's on the run from the police.

PANTALAIMON. Let's go.

LYRA. No, don't. It's good, in a way. It means we can trust him. And . . . it's moving again. It's telling me something I never even asked it.

PANTALAIMON. What?

LYRA. It says I gotta stop looking for Roger. I gotta stay with Will. I gotta help him find what he's lookin' for. That's my task.

Geneva. The Consistorial Court of Discipline. MRS COULTER, LORD BOREAL *and* FRA PAVEL *are there with the* PRESIDENT. BROTHER JASPER *sits quietly, taking notes.*

PRESIDENT. 'It is the name of one who came before . . . you have always feared her . . . now she has come again.' Thank you, Mrs Coulter, for having persuaded the witch to tell you.

LORD BOREAL. It was a painful process.

FRA PAVEL. To harden one's heart is the first step to holiness.

PRESIDENT. I don't agree. As President of the Consistorial Court of Discipline, it is my task to seek out and to punish all those who would threaten the Church. The suffering that Mrs Coulter inflicted on that poor damned creature was nothing compared to the tortures that I authorise every day. But I have never once hardened my heart. I feel the lash on the heretic's back as keenly as he does. I do it to save his soul. I do it for love.

MRS COULTER. My feelings exactly, Father President. As for my daughter . . . All I am asking for, is permission to find her. Once she's safely in my care, you can leave it to me to discover the truth about her.

FRA PAVEL. Then what would be the point of the alethiometer?

MRS COULTER. I've been wondering that myself. It's thrown no light on the secret name or anything else. The fact is, Father President, and I speak as a devout believer, that the Church has had chance after chance to find my daughter, and it's made a complete and utter mess of every one of them. Can you not trust her mother to track her down?

FRA PAVEL. So you can do the Church's job better than it can itself?

LORD BOREAL. If I may . . . ? With all respect, at any normal time, the Church would do the job very well. But this is no normal time. Lord Asriel has broken through the Aurora into a different world and, if reports are to be believed, he plans to kill the Authority. Should we not be grateful for Mrs Coulter's help at a time like this?

FRA PAVEL. Let's not exaggerate . . .

MRS COULTER. Exaggerate!

FRA PAVEL. . . . There was, as we all know, a similar attack on the Authority many thousands of years ago and it failed quite miserably. There's no reason to think that Lord Asriel can do any better.

LORD BOREAL. There's *every* reason! That first rebellion only failed because the Authority could not be harmed by any weapon that existed at that time. But I've discovered on my travels, that such a weapon has since been made.

PRESIDENT. Go on.

LORD BOREAL. It is a knife of astonishing sharpness. It can cut through air. It can cut through spirit with ease. It could kill the Authority. And if Lord Asriel finds it . . .

PRESIDENT. Fra Pavel, why have I not been told about this knife? Does Lord Asriel know about it? And how can we get to it first?

FRA PAVEL. I shall ask the alethiometer. But I'm afraid that three whole questions, where one alone can take up to a year to answer . . .

PRESIDENT. I've heard enough. Lord Boreal, since it is you who has made this claim, you will find this knife, and bring it here to Geneva.

LORD BOREAL. Oh, but I can't! No adult can. It's in a city thronged with Spectres who, believe it or not, devour the souls of fully-grown humans. But a child could get it . . . a boy, a boy who can fight . . . a boy who can kill . . . and I know of a boy who can. His name is Will. Will Parry.

PRESIDENT. Find him and send him.

MRS COULTER. And my daughter, Father President?

PRESIDENT. You may search for her. If you find her, you will tell us at once. There is one further matter.

He lays a hand gently on BROTHER JASPER*'s shoulder.*

Am I right in believing that you can read the alethiometer?

FRA PAVEL (*who wasn't watching*). *Read* it? I'm the world's acknowledged expert!

PRESIDENT. I was speaking to Brother Jasper.

BROTHER JASPER. I read it well, Father President. I have a gift for it. I'm said to have had an angel ancestor, perhaps that's the reason.

PRESIDENT. Fra Pavel, give him yours.

FRA PAVEL I beg your pardon?

PRESIDENT (*angry*). Give him yours!

Reluctantly, FRA PAVEL *does.*

BROTHER JASPER. Where shall I start?

PRESIDENT. Begin with Lyra. Ask it about the secret name. That above all is my concern. Dear friends, good day. Fra Pavel, wait in your study. You will shortly receive a visit.

Cittàgazze window. WILL *and* LYRA, *looking.*

LYRA. I can't see anything that even *looks* like a window.

WILL. Maybe it's gone.

LYRA. No, look.

The window appears. Traffic is heard.

Oh, Will! It's wonderful. Only . . . what's that noise?

WILL. It's the traffic on the Oxford ring road.

LYRA *looks through.*

Don't stand in front, or they'll see your legs.

LYRA. I don't mind if they see my legs.

WILL. But there won't be a body, will there? Just two legs with nothing on top, and that'll *really* freak them out. Get down and look from one side. And put that daemon of yours in your pocket.

She does.

LYRA. Are you sure it's Oxford? It don't look like any bit of Oxford *I* know.

WILL. Yes! Now jump through quickly and move away fast as you can.

LYRA *goes through. There's the blare of a horn and a screech of brakes.*

Watch out!

He dashes through after her.

Are you all right?

They're in WILL's *Oxford. We see a variety of* ORDINARY PEOPLE.

LYRA. I'm fine. I wasn't expecting it all to be so busy.

WILL. This isn't busy. It's just people and cars. Let's move on, there's someone looking.

They do.

LYRA. Maybe I better stick with you for a bit.

WILL. Well, just don't talk to anyone. Not one word. You got that?

LYRA. Yeah, all right.

She stares around in amazement.

All these people, and not one of 'em's got a daemon!

WILL. Stop staring.

They walk on.

LYRA. What's them white dots on the pavement?

WILL. Chewing gum. Don't ask.

She approaches someone waiting at the bus shelter.

LYRA. Excuse me. Is this the way to the centre of town?

WILL *pulls* LYRA *away.*

WILL. *Never* do that again.

LYRA. What you talking about?

WILL. You were calling attention to yourself. You gotta keep quiet and still, then people won't notice you. Look, just believe me, Lyra, I've been doing it all my life. You're not being serious.

LYRA. Serious? I'm the best liar there ever was. I lie and shout and make a big show, and I sort of . . . hide behind it. And I don't get caught, not ever. You're the one who's not being serious. You're meant to be hiding from the police, and you en't got the first idea.

WILL. Who said I'm hiding from the police?

LYRA. You are though, aren't you? 'Cause you murdered someone.

WILL. Let's go in here where it's not so busy.

The Botanic Gardens. The tree and bench are there.

LYRA. Will! It's the Botanic Gardens. We got one in my Oxford too, just the same. *Exactly* the same.

WILL. Sit down.

    LYRA *does.*

    How did you know about me?

LYRA. I asked this.

    She produces the alethiometer.

    It's an alethiometer. I ask it whatever I want to know, and it tells me.

WILL. You were spying on me!

LYRA. I wasn't! Well, not much. 'Cause then it told me to forget everything what I was plannin' to do, and help you instead. And I hate that. It makes me really angry. But it's what it said, an' I can't say no, so what're you lookin' for? Tell me.

WILL. I'm looking for my father. He went to the Arctic on
an expedition when I was still a baby, and he vanished.
His name was John, John Parry. A soldier. And when I got
older . . . these men started hanging about the house, and
telephoning my mum. She said they were spooks . . . like . . .
secret-service people.

LYRA. What did they want?

WILL. This.

He shows her the green leather writing-case. Opens it.

It's got my father's letters inside, that he wrote from the
Arctic. The spooks kept on hassling us to get them, and my
mother got ill, so I took her to stay with a friend. And that
same night, I woke up to hear two men inside the house.
Rummaging round and whispering. I hid behind a door at
the top of the stairs . . . and one of them came up, very
slowly, an' he stopped . . . an' I ran out and crashed into
him. Hilarious really, a kid like me attacking a trained killer.
Except that Moxie, my cat, was just behind him. Here.

He gestures to the back of his knees.

And he tipped right over her and crashed down the stairs.
And he was dead. I grabbed this case and ran, an' that's
when I came to Oxford. 'Cause there's books here, and
libraries and newspaper offices. And I can find out all about
my father. This is the last letter he wrote. He's up in the
Arctic, and he's found an 'anomaly'. Something peculiar.
He's put the directions down, longitude, latitude, everything.
It's at a place called Lookout Ridge, and there's a rock
that's shaped like an eagle.

LYRA. An' what's the anom . . . the anomaly?

WILL. That's what I wanna find out.

LYRA. I'll help you, Will.

WILL. You can if you like, but I don't want you using that
machine of yours. It's like finding out secrets about me.
Things I don't tell anyone.

LYRA. All right, I won't.

WILL. Why should I trust you?

LYRA. I told you about my friend Roger. Only I didn't tell you everything. I thought I was saving his life, and instead I took him to the most dangerous place he could have been. And now he's dead. I'll never betray a friend again, I promise.

She gives him the alethiometer in its bag.

Take this. Just for today. It's the most precious thing I got. It means that I trust *you*.

He takes it.

WILL. And you take this.

He gives her the writing-case.

I'll meet you back here.

WILL's *Oxford.* LORD BOREAL *approaches the desk of a cuttings library. The* LIBRARIAN *is there, with an* ASSISTANT. WILL *is at a table, keeping tight hold of the alethiometer-bag. He reads and makes notes.*

LORD BOREAL. Good morning.

LIBRARIAN. Good morning, sir. We haven't seen you in the library for quite some weeks.

LORD BOREAL. I've been away. I sent a message about some cuttings I wish to read.

ASSISTANT (*to the* LIBRARIAN). I'm looking them up right now, sir.

LORD BOREAL. Only now? I did explain that it was urgent.

ASSISTANT. Was it 'P-A-double R-Y,' sir?

LORD BOREAL. 'Parry', that is correct. Major John Parry.

ASSISTANT. That's odd. One of the files is out already. It must be with that young lad over there. He said he was doing some research for a school project.

LIBRARIAN. Well, get it off him!

LORD BOREAL *sees* WILL.

LORD BOREAL. Please . . . do no such thing. I'd hate to think that I was stunting his education. And bring me the rest.

He approaches WILL.

Would you mind if I shared your table?

WILL *nods while trying to look unnoticeable.*

I do admire you young people. You know exactly the information that you want, and where to find it. May I?

He takes a cutting and reads from it.

'ARCHEOLOGICAL EXPEDITION VANISHES.' This was the Nuniatak dig, was it not? I remember it well. There were scientists, geologists and a military advisor. But of course you'd know that.

Slowly, WILL *turns to face him.*

WILL. Why?

LORD BOREAL. Because the military advisor was your father. I had a shrewd suspicion that you'd want to read about his adventures. But I didn't expect to find you quite so soon.

WILL *glances at the door in panic.*

Don't be afraid. I won't give you away unless you force me to.

The ASSISTANT *approaches.*

Are those for me?

ASSISTANT. That's right, sir. The lad's not bothering you, I hope?

LORD BOREAL. Not at all! We're getting acquainted, aren't we, Will?

The ASSISTANT *moves away.*

Oh yes, I know your name. I know your face, from the records that my friends in the secret services have been keeping on you. I know why you're on the run. I knew the man you killed.

WILL. What do you want?

LORD BOREAL. Lower your voice, and listen carefully. I need to send you on an errand. It's a difficult one and it may require you to kill again. I strongly advise you to do as I say. Or would you rather I had you arrested?

WILL. You won't though, will you? 'Cause if I was arrested, I wouldn't be any use to you. So sod off.

LORD BOREAL *smiles.*

LORD BOREAL. That's a very good answer. Do get in touch, if you change your mind. I'll leave my card.

He does.

Oh, by the way. There's something here that I think might interest you.

He produces a cutting from his wallet and reads.

'LEGENDS OF THE ARCTIC by Major John Parry.'

WILL. Give it to me!

LORD BOREAL. Don't be impatient, Will.

He skims on.

. . . Yes, here we are. 'In a place unknown, near a rock in the shape of an eagle, is a strange anomaly: a doorway into the spirit-world. Only the bravest warriors dared to enter. None had returned.'

He gives WILL *the cutting.*

'None had returned.' Good day.

WILL *reads the cutting with single-minded interest.* LORD BOREAL *takes the alethiometer-bag and leaves.*

Cittàgazze. In the mountains. JOPARI *is tracing a large circle with his staff. He is ill but mentally vigorous.* LEE SCORESBY *is there.*

JOPARI (*calls upwards*). Witches! Come down to rest for a moment.

He sits exhausted. The WITCHES *descend to earth. Meanwhile:*

LEE SCORESBY. Is this the world that the little gal came to?

JOPARI. It is. And it's the world that I first arrived in when I left my home. I was looking for a window in the air, like the one that we've just flown through. But the snow was so thick, and the blizzard so blinding, that I walked right through it without even knowing it was there. I never found it again. So I made a new life for myself, of a different kind. (*To the* WITCHES.) Welcome to Cittàgazze!

CAITLIN. We can breathe.

GRIMHILD. But the air feels different.

PIPISTRELLE. When we flew through the clouds, even the rain felt different on our faces.

JOPARI. Stay in the circle! You'll be safe inside it for a moment or two until the charm wears off. After that, you'll be food for the Spectres, just like any short-lived mortal.

He points.

Do you see them now? Drifting, shimmering, like smoke in a mirror. They've multiplied like flies since I saw them last. You must go. Good luck to you all, as you search for your child of destiny. Serafina, you will not see me again. I am dying. Farewell.

SERAFINA. Farewell.

The WITCHES *go.*

LEE SCORESBY. It's a dangerous world those gals have come to.

JOPARI. They'll be safe enough as long as they keep to the air. And so shall I. That's why I called you, Mr Scoresby.

LEE SCORESBY. You called me nowhere, you old witch-doctor. I came to you of my own free will.

JOPARI. You came to me because of a dream. I sent you that dream. I needed you and your power of flight to take me further on, to a city beside the sea.

LEE SCORESBY. I never signed up to be no cab driver!

JOPARI. This is important. In a tower they call the Tower of Angels, there's a man named Giacomo Paradisi. He's old and frail, but when he was young he fought for a knife, and won it. Now he must take that knife on a long and perilous journey. I must give him that order before I die. And you must take me to him in your balloon.

LEE SCORESBY. Will it be good for Lyra?

JOPARI. It will be good.

LEE SCORESBY. Then let's hit the trail.

WILL*'s Oxford.* LYRA *and* WILL *are there.*

LYRA. How could you let him *steal* it? I can't do *nothing* without it. Nothing! I can't find Roger. I can't know nothing about what my mother's up to . . .

WILL. Look, I said I was sorry. He distracted me. He showed me something that my father had written.

He stops.

LYRA. *What*?

WILL. I've just remembered something. He left his card. I've got his address.

He takes out LORD BOREAL*'s visiting card.*

Sir Charles Latrom, Limefield House, Headington, Oxford.

LYRA. Good. Let's burgle him.

WILL. We can't.

LYRA. Iorek Byrnison would.

WILL. Yeah, I would too, if I was a ten-foot bear. Lyra, there'll be wires and alarms and lights flashing all over the place.

LYRA. So what we gonna do?

WILL. We'll go and see him.

They have arrived at LORD BOREAL's *front door.* WILL *and* LYRA *knock on the door.* LORD BOREAL *appears.*

LORD BOREAL. Will Parry? I've been expecting you.

LYRA *and* LORD BOREAL *recognise each other.*

And Lyra Belacqua! This is a surprise!

LYRA. Lord Boreal! How did you get here?

LORD BOREAL. Did you really suppose that you were the only person to travel between the worlds? I've been coming to this one very much longer than you. 'Latrom', of course, is a name that I chose for my private amusement. Shall we talk business?

WILL. There's nothing to talk about. You stole something that belongs to Lyra, and we want it back.

LORD BOREAL. Is it this?

He takes the alethiometer out of his pocket.

LYRA. Give it to me!

LORD BOREAL. Oh no, not yet. I had assumed, Master Parry, that the bag you were clutching in the reading room was the case of letters that my friends in the secret services here are so anxious to find. Instead, I discovered this curious object. It would sit very nicely in my collection of antique instruments . . . but its value for me is reckoned entirely in

the heartbroken look on Lyra's face as I hold it in front of
her. I have a bargaining chip.

WILL. Give it back to us.

LORD BOREAL. I'll happily do so, but on one condition. You
see, there's something else that I want much more.

LYRA. Get it yourself!

LORD BOREAL. I can't. It's in a place where only children
can survive. Lyra, I know you've been there. Go back, and
look for a tower with stone angels carved around the
doorway. In that tower, there is a knife. I must have that
knife. Master Parry, you'll need to fight the Bearer to get it
off him. But he's an elderly man, he'll be no match for a
hardened murderer like yourself. Bring me that knife and
Lyra will get her toy back. Return without it, and I shall call
the police. Now off you go.

WILL *and* LYRA *leave.*

Cittàgazze. The Torre degli Angeli. LYRA, WILL *and*
PANTALAIMON *look at it.*

An old man, GIACOMO PARADISI, *is at the top of the tower,
fighting over a knife with an agile young man: this is* TULLIO.
PARADISI *is bloodied and wounded.* TULLIO *grabs the knife
off* PARADISI *and disappears to descend down the interior of
the tower.*

PARADISI. You down there! Run! Run! He's taken the knife!

WILL *moves to get away.*

WILL. Let's go.

LYRA. Where're you goin'? You gotta stay an' fight.

WILL. You serious?

LYRA. 'Course I'm serious! It was you that lost the
alethiometer, so you gotta get it back.

WILL. But he's got the knife an' I've got nothing.

TULLIO rushes out of the door. He sees WILL and threatens him with the knife.

LYRA. If you don't, I will!

She rushes at TULLIO.

TULLIO. Get away! I'll kill you!

WILL pulls LYRA away and turns to face TULLIO. They fight. At first, WILL fares badly. Then he starts to fight dirtily and with determination, and wins possession of the knife. TULLIO looks around in terror.

Give it back! Please! You don't need it! You're just a kid!

LYRA. Come on!

She drags WILL into the tower, and they climb the stairs unseen. TULLIO sees the SPECTRES approaching him. He waves his arms in the air, as though fending off a cloud of bats. He turns to the wall of the tower and inspects it closely. Finally he stands frozen and immobile. LYRA and WILL appear on the roof of the tower.

Was that the Bearer?

PARADISI. No, I am the Bearer. He stole the knife from me and, like a fool, he thought that he could use it.

He takes the knife and calls down to TULLIO.

Only the Bearer can use it!

LYRA. Will! Your fingers! He's cut off your fingers!

WILL looks at his hand. His little finger and the one next to it have been cut off. PARADISI sees this.

PARADISI. You've won the knife. When I was a boy, I fought and won it, just like you. You see?

He shows his hand, from which two fingers have been severed like WILL's.

These missing fingers are the badge of the Bearer. Now it has passed to you.

He offers WILL *the knife.*

WILL. Look, the only reason I got mixed up in this is because of a man who wants the knife for himself.

PARADISI. I know the man you mean. Don't give him the knife. He will betray you. Take it.

WILL. No!

PARADISI. With this knife, you can cut windows between the worlds.

For the first time, WILL *wants the knife.*

Take it.

WILL *takes the knife.*

Its name is 'Æsahættr'. Hold it ahead of you.

WILL *holds out the knife.*

Now feel. You're looking for a snag, a gap so small you'd never see it, but the tip will find it, if you put your mind there.

WILL. I'm feeling sick.

PARADISI. Relax. Don't force it. The knife is subtle. Place your mind where the edge is sharpest. *Be* the tip of the knife.

WILL. I can feel . . . the snag.

PARADISI. Now think of nothing else. If for a single moment your thoughts should waver, the knife will break. Tease the point into the heart of the snag . . . and cut.

WILL *cuts. A window opens. Traffic is heard.*

LYRA. It's Oxford.

PARADISI. Now you must learn to close the window. That's my last lesson. Then I shall wait on this rooftop, out of the Spectres' range, until I die.

He shows WILL, *using his fingertips.*

Feel for the edge, just as you felt with the knife. Put your whole soul into the tips of your fingers. Then . . . pinch it.

WILL *tries.* LYRA *and* PARADISI *watch. The traffic noise continues.*

WILL. I can't. Just can't.

LYRA. You're trying to shut out the pain. You gotta accept it.

WILL. All right, I'll try.

He tries, and pinches the window closed. The traffic noise stops.

PARADISI. Now you are the Bearer. You can slice the air and heal it. You can travel between the worlds. You can prevail against men, monsters, spirits, spectres, even the most high angels. And in the war that is to come, you may be called to aim it even higher.

*

SERAFINA *and the* WITCHES *appear in the sky.*

SERAFINA. Look sisters! Angels!

She looks through her amber spyglass.

Angels whirling and swooping in battalions, just as they did all those aeons ago when they made war on the Authority and were defeated.

GRENDELLA. There was no Lyra then, and no Lord Asriel.

SERAFINA. You think it's possible, then, that they could win this time?

WITCHES. Yes! / The Church will fall! / The Authority will die! / Dust will triumph! / Fly on! / Fly on to Lyra!

*

LORD ASRIEL *appears in his fortress.*

LORD ASRIEL. 'Into this wild abyss the wary fiend
Stood on the brink of Hell and looked a while
Pondering his voyage.'

*

MRS COULTER *appears with the* GOLDEN MONKEY.

MRS COULTER. Lyra, where are you?

*

On the tower.

WILL. Father! I'm coming to find you!

*

The PRESIDENT *appears.* BROTHER JASPER *meets him.*

BROTHER JASPER. Father President.

PRESIDENT. Well?

BROTHER JASPER. I have discovered Lyra Belacqua's secret
name.

He hands the PRESIDENT *a sheet of paper. The* PRESIDENT
reads it.

End of Part One.

PART TWO

CHARACTERS IN PART TWO

Between the Worlds

LORD ASRIEL *and* STELMARIA
MRS COULTER *and the* GOLDEN MONKEY
LYRA BELACQUA *and* PANTALAIMON
WILL *and* KIRJAVA
LORD BOREAL
JOPARI

THE CHURCH
THE PRESIDENT
BROTHER JASPER *and* PERPETUA

WITCHES
SERAFINA PEKKALA *and* KAISA
RUTA SKADI
GRIMHILD
PIPISTRELLE
CAITLIN
GRENDELLA

GALLIVESPIANS
LORD ROKE
THE CHEVALIER TIALYS
THE LADY SALMAKIA

BEARS
IOREK BYRNISON

ANGELS
BALTHAMOS
BARUCH

Cittàgazze

ANGELICA
PAOLO
GIACOMO PARADISI

The Land of the Dead

MR PERKINS, *an official*
JEPTHA JONES
HANNAH JONES
OLD MOTHER JONES
MOTHER JONES'S DEATH
LYRA'S DEATH
THE BOATMAN
NO-NAME, *a harpy*
ROGER PARSLOW

WITCHES, CLERICS, BEARS, GHOSTS, TARTAR GUARDS,
SOLDIERS, HARPIES *and others*

ACT ONE

Opening montage.

LYRA *and* PANTALAIMON *are running.*

LYRA. Run, Pan! Run!

*

LORD ASRIEL *and* MRS COULTER *are there.*

LORD ASRIEL. Look at that pathway! Look at the sun . . . it's the light of another world! Don't turn your back on it, Marisa. Come with me. We'll smash the universe into pieces, and put it together in a new way. Isn't that what you want? To be part of my plan?

MRS COULTER *pulls away from him.*

MRS COULTER. I can't.

*

ROGER *is dying.*

ROGER. Feel funny.

LYRA *embraces him.*

LYRA. Roger! Rodge!

*

SERAFINA *addresses the witches.*

SERAFINA. Sisters, listen to me! The prophecy has begun, and the child is amongst us. And now the Church is after her . . . !

WITCHES. Do they know her name?

SERAFINA. Not yet! That's still our secret. And now we must find her and keep her from harm until her destiny's run its course.

*

LYRA *meets* WILL.

LYRA. Where is it? Where you come from?

WILL. No, you wouldn't believe it.

LYRA. I might.

WILL. All right. I come from a different world.

LYRA. Well . . . So do I. ·

*

MRS COULTER *is putting her case to the* PRESIDENT.

MRS COULTER. All I am asking for, Father President, is permission to find my daughter. Once she's safely in my care, you can leave it to me to discover the truth about her.

PRESIDENT. You may search for her. But if you find her, you must tell us at once.

MRS COULTER. Of course!

*

WILL *and* LYRA *are together.*

WILL. I'm looking for my father. He went to the Arctic on an expedition when I was still a baby, and he vanished. His name was John, John Parry.

*

JOPARI *appears with* LEE SCORESBY.

JOPARI. In that tower is a man named Giacomo Paradisi. He's old and frail, but when he was young, he fought for the knife and won it. Now he must take that knife on a long and perilous journey.

LEE SCORESBY. Will it be good for Lyra?

JOPARI. It will be good.

*

LYRA *watches as* WILL *and* TULLIO *fight.* WILL *wins.*

LYRA. Will! Your hand!

*

RUTA SKADI *confronts* SERAFINA PEKKALA.

SERAFINA. So where will you go, while we fly onwards?

RUTA SKADI. I'll fly to the battlefield, to fight for Lord
Asriel. When you see Jopari, tell him I've not forgotten that
he rejected me. If I see him, I'll kill him.

*

BROTHER JASPER *approaches the* PRESIDENT.

BROTHER JASPER. Father President.

PRESIDENT. Well?

BROTHER JASPER. I have discovered Lyra Belacqua's secret
name.

He hands the PRESIDENT *a document. The* PRESIDENT
reads it.

PRESIDENT. Summon the Council!

Bells toll. CHURCH DIGNITARIES *assemble in the
Consistorial Court of Discipline.* BROTHER JASPER *is there.
The* PRESIDENT *addresses the conclave.*

PRESIDENT. Princes of the Church, we face the gravest
possible crisis. Brother Jasper, our new alethiometer-reader,
will tell you what he has learned. You will debate it and
help me determine what should be done. I shall not speak.

He motions to BROTHER JASPER, *who takes the floor.*

BROTHER JASPER. Ever since Lyra Belacqua was born, it
has been known that she's the child in the witches' prophecy,
the child who will either redeem the Church or bring about
the triumph of Dust, one or the other. The answer to this
riddle could be found only in a secret name . . . which the
alethiometer has now revealed. That name is Eve, the fount
of original sin and the cause of Dust's invasion of the world.
The Triumph of Dust!

HARDBALL CLERIC. Father President, this is *not* the major crisis.

SOFTBALL CLERIC. I agree.

HARDBALL CLERIC. Brother Jasper here has raised a problem, which *may* affect us at some time in the future. What's happening *now* is that Lord Asriel is planning to kill the Authority. *That's* what we have to deal with.

FERVENT CLERIC. So Dust takes over the world while we ignore it?

HARDBALL CLERIC. I'm not convinced that it will.

SOFTBALL CLERIC. I'm not convinced that Brother Jasper has read the alethiometer correctly. I think he's young and over-enthusiastic and he's got carried away. I also feel that this obsession with children and Dust is taking us back to the worst excesses of the General Oblation Board!

HARDBALL CLERIC. How do we know that this so-called prophecy isn't just some superstitious twaddle dreamed up by the witches?

FERVENT CLERIC. Disgraceful!

WILY CLERIC. Speaking on behalf of the Society of the Holy Spirit, I think it might help if we knew what Lord Asriel was actually doing.

The HARDBALL CLERIC *sighs with impatience.*

HARDBALL CLERIC. I'll spell it out. He is building a fortress. He is constructing weapons of awesome potential. He's issued a rallying call to malcontents throughout the universe, angels included.

WILY CLERIC. But will the angels join him?

HARDBALL CLERIC. They certainly will. They're still smarting from the last rebellion.

FERVENT CLERIC. They're smarting because they were soundly thrashed! And their leader was cast into eternal perdition, and *that* will be Lord Asriel's fate, you mark my words!

HARDBALL CLERIC. But there's a knife this time. The subtle knife. Æsahættr. It can kill the Authority just as surely as though he was a human being. I propose that we attack Lord Asriel *now*, before he gets it.

SOFTBALL CLERIC. But I wonder . . . is it quite wise to rush into a war, before we know who's got the ultimate weapon? What if we find ourselves on the losing side?

FERVENT CLERIC. Are you suggesting that the Authority could be defeated?

SOFTBALL CLERIC. If Lord Asriel gets the knife, then yes, he very well could.

WILY CLERIC. I must point out that we don't yet know if the Authority really needs our help. He hasn't asked for it.

SOFTBALL CLERIC. He hasn't talked to anyone since . . . would it be Saint Teresa?

WILY CLERIC. Teresa the Seventh. My point is this. When war breaks out, it will be angels fighting angels in the heights of heaven. And heavenly matters aren't our first concern. We guard the Church on earth. We guard its borders, we guard its power, we guard its wealth. And it's our duty, it seems to me, to have the wherewithal to do just that, and nothing more.

FERVENT CLERIC. Are you seriously saying that we ought to wait till we see who's got the knife, before we decide what side we're on?

SOFTBALL CLERIC. No, that's what *I* was saying. What His Reverence here is saying, is that we should get the knife for ourselves, and then hang on to it.

FERVENT CLERIC. Saints preserve us!

WILY CLERIC. Well, it would guarantee the Church's power for a thousand years. What would be wrong with that?

SOFTBALL CLERIC. It might look opportunistic.

WILY CLERIC. How it would *look*, of course, is very important. Our brethren in the colonies would be very upset indeed if they thought we were cooking up some kind of compromise.

FERVENT CLERIC. And rightly so!

THE PRESIDENT *stands.*

PRESIDENT. You are all dismissed!

They file out. As they go:

HARDBALL CLERIC. That went very well. We'll be at war before we know it.

WILY CLERIC. I think we may.

They have gone.

PRESIDENT (*to* BROTHER JASPER). They understand nothing of Dust. Nothing of Eve. Nothing of what must be done. Come closer.

BROTHER JASPER *does.*

Find out where Lyra is hiding.

BROTHER JASPER. And then?

PRESIDENT. I want you to gather a band of warriors. Young men like you, pure in heart and ready to die for the sacred cause. Young men who can kill. They will receive their orders later. Go in peace.

The air over Cittàgazze. The WITCHES *are flying.*

SERAFINA. Fly on, sisters!

PIPISTRELLE. I've seen no sign of the child.

WITCHES. Nor me! / Nor me!

SERAFINA. But she's here in Cittàgazze. That we know. Jopari told us. Fly on!

WITCHES. Fly on! Fly on!

Oxford. Night. WILL *and* LYRA *at the iron gate to* LORD BOREAL'*s house. It's locked shut.* LYRA *rattles the gate.*

LYRA. What do you think?

WILL. Let's try.

He uses the knife to cut through the gate, and they go through.

LYRA. Look, there's the house, and there en't any lights on, so he's gotta be out.

WILL. Hang on.

LYRA. Is your hand still hurting?

WILL. Yes, and it's bleeding like anything. Do up the bandage, will you?

She starts doing so.

LYRA. I did this.

WILL. Yeah, well, shut up about it.

LYRA. I did. You'd never have fought that man if I hadn't pushed you into it. 'Cause I wanted the alethiometer back, and I shouldn't've have done. I'm meant to be helping you find your dad.

WILL. Well, you forgot for a minute. Let's get on with what we're doing.

LYRA. We don't have to. We could knock on Lord Boreal's door and give him the knife, like we said we was going to.

WILL. Then he'll have *both* our things. Look, it's all decided. We'll keep the knife, and burgle his house and take back the alethiometer.

LYRA. How?

WILL. You stay here. Then I'll cut a window from this world into Cittàgazze, and I'll walk to where I think his study is, cut into it and grab the alethiometer, then I'll jump back into Cittàgazze-world, run back here, you come through, and I'll close up the window. Got it?

LYRA. You're gonna cut into another world, walk along a bit and cut back into this one?

WILL. Yeah.

LYRA. While I stay here?

WILL. That's it. Don't bother me now. If I think about anything else, the knife's gonna break, remember? And Pan, you better do your mouse act again.

PANTALAIMON. I was expecting that.

He turns into a mouse.

WILL. Take this.

He gives LYRA *the green leather writing-case and cuts a window.*

I won't be a minute.

He goes through. MRS COULTER *is heard approaching.*

MRS COULTER. Through here?

LYRA. Will!

LYRA *goes through the window after him.* LORD BOREAL *and* MRS COULTER *appear.*

MRS COULTER. So this is your secret world? It's charming, Charles.

LORD BOREAL. I hardly believe its charm is what made you insist that I brought you here.

MRS COULTER. Of course it isn't. I want my daughter. Will I be sharing a room with her?

LORD BOREAL. No, certainly not. I've asked my manservant to make up the guest room for you.

MRS COULTER. The guest room? Well, we mustn't upset him. I must remember to rumple the sheets in the morning. You really are the most delightfully old-fashioned host.

They have reached the front door.

LORD BOREAL. After you.

They go into the house. WILL *appears, peering down through a knife-made window in the ceiling of* LORD BOREAL*'s study.* LYRA *appears.*

LYRA. Will!

WILL. What are you doing? I told you to stay outside.

LYRA. He's back, and he's brought my mum! If she finds me, I'm done for!

She sees the window.

Where are we anyway? Why's the window pointing downwards?

WILL. It's the only way I could cut in. The ground level here must be lower or something.

LYRA. Yeah, that's right . . . 'cause it's a different world, so the hills and valleys can all be different too.

WILL. Let's hope they don't look up at the ceiling.

LYRA. Well, at least we en't poking up through the floor.

LORD BOREAL *is heard outside the study.*

LORD BOREAL. Leave your bags in the room on the left.

WILL. Ssh!

LORD BOREAL *comes into the study. He puts away the alethiometer.*

LYRA. He's got the alethiometer!

LORD BOREAL *opens a drawer, takes out a revolver, checks it and puts it back.*

Look!

The GOLDEN MONKEY *bounds in, followed by* MRS COULTER.

MRS COULTER. And just what do you do in this world, exactly?

LORD BOREAL. Very much as I do at home. I cultivate prize orchids, I collect antiques and I have a not-too-stressful posting with the secret services. May I offer you a glass of sherry?

MRS COULTER. Thank you.

LORD BOREAL *pours sherry. Meanwhile:*

Now you are quite certain that Lyra's coming?

LORD BOREAL. Without a doubt. She wants her pretty piece of clockwork.

MRS COULTER. You won't *really* give it back to her, will you?

LORD BOREAL. Oh, no. Although I'm sure she'll scream and shout and cause an appalling scene.

MRS COULTER. She'll learn to behave when I've got her under lock and key, I can assure you of that.

LYRA (*to* WILL). Bloody old cow.

MRS COULTER. I shall *never* forgive you for sending her into that terrible Spectre-world.

LORD BOREAL. She's in no danger. Children are safer in Cittàgazze than anywhere else.

MRS COULTER. Children aren't normally sent there to fight for deadly weapons. What if they both get killed?

LORD BOREAL. Marisa, my dear, if there's a boy in the universe who can win that knife, it's him. Will Parry.

LYRA (*to* WILL). Yeah.

WILL *shows* LYRA *his wounded hand.*

WILL. Yeah but.

MRS COULTER. How can you be so sure?

LORD BOREAL. Because he's a murderer.

MRS COULTER. A *murderer*?

LORD BOREAL. My dear, he's twelve years old, and he's already killed a highly-trained secret-service operative. Oh yes, a very bad hat. On drugs, I imagine . . . single mother living on state handouts . . .

WILL. You bastard!

MRS COULTER. Yes, well, that's typical of Lyra. Even at Jordan, she used to find her playmates in the gutter. We had one of them at Bolvangar, a beastly little kitchen boy, called Roddy or Rudy . . .

LYRA. I'll kill her!

WILL. Calm down! I want you to go back into Oxford, come round the outside of the house and chuck a couple of stones at the window, so they go running outside, all right? I'll grab the alethiometer and run.

LYRA. Yeah, all right. But I'm still gonna kill her.

She goes.

MRS COULTER. But she's my daughter, Charles. And I insist on absolute frankness about your dealings with her.

LORD BOREAL. Don't you trust me?

MRS COULTER. No, I don't. You're keeping something back, it's obvious. Will Parry may well be a thug and hooligan, that I believe. But there are thousands of boys like that. Why was it him, and *only* him, who could get you the knife? What makes him different?

LORD BOREAL. The blood in his veins.

WILL *wiggles as far down as he can into the room to hear this.*

MRS COULTER. What do you mean?

LORD BOREAL. Twelve years ago, Will's father, John Parry, discovered a window between the worlds. He walked through, and found himself in Cittàgazze. My friends in the secret services have been trying to find that window for years. It has profound intelligence implications . . .

MRS COULTER. Stick to the father.

LORD BOREAL. I shall. Parry is still alive, in hiding, under a different name, the name that was given to him by the Northern tribesmen.

MRS COULTER. And what makes him so remarkable?

LORD BOREAL *is about to reply when a handful of stones clatters against a glass window.*

It's them, it must be!

LORD BOREAL *takes the revolver out of the drawer.*

Charles! What are you doing?

He runs out. WILL *prepares to climb down into the room.* LORD BOREAL *appears in the garden.* LYRA *can be seen, searching for the window into Cittàgazze.* LORD BOREAL *calls:*

LORD BOREAL. Will? Will, are you there?

MRS COULTER *appears after him.*

MRS COULTER. Put that gun away this instant!

LORD BOREAL. It's just for the boy. Only the boy. (*Calls.*) Don't worry, Will, I'm not going to harm you.

MRS COULTER *moves further into the garden, calling:*

MRS COULTER. Lyra? Lyra?

LYRA. Go away!

MRS COULTER. Don't be afraid, my darling! I'll look after you!

LYRA. Will! Where are you?

WILL *appears in the Cittàgazze window, carrying the alethiometer.* LORD BOREAL *raises his gun to fire. The* GOLDEN MONKEY *leaps at him and the gun fires into the air.*

WILL. Lyra! Over here!

He pulls LYRA *through and closes the window.* LORD BOREAL *and* MRS COULTER *stare at the place where the window disappeared.*

MRS COULTER. We've got to go after them.

LORD BOREAL. Marisa, we can't! They've gone into Cittàgazze!

MRS COULTER. They can have gone into hell for all I care. I haven't come all this way, to be satisfied with a glimpse of my daughter by a clump of palm trees.

LORD BOREAL. But the Spectres will kill us!

MRS COULTER. *Will* you be quiet? You've told me about the Spectres, and . . . I'm sure of it . . . there must be a way of getting control of them. It's to do with adults and children, isn't it? . . . and Dust . . . and everything I was working on at Bolvangar. Yes, I can do it.

LORD BOREAL. Go on your own! Let me stay here!

She laughs.

MRS COULTER. Have you forgotten your orders, Charles? You're getting the knife. And the knife is *there*.

She points to where the window appeared.

We'll leave in the morning.

Cittàgazze. WILL *lies collapsed on the ground, exhausted and in pain.* LYRA *is with him.*

WILL. He was talking about my father. He said he found a window. Just like me. And he's *alive*.

LYRA. Are you all right, Will?

WILL. I'm just tired.

LYRA. Ssh . . . Let's talk in the morning. We'll go to the place we met. I'll cook an omelette . . .

WILL *is asleep.*

He's asleep.

PANTALAIMON. Why do you think his father's so important?

LYRA. Dunno.

PANTALAIMON. Where d'you think he is?

LYRA. I don't know!

PANTALAIMON. You could ask the alethiometer.

LYRA. Oh Pan, you heard what he said in Oxford. I can't go
snooping on him.

PANTALAIMON. That makes a change. It used to be you who
was always snooping, and me who tried to stop you.

LYRA. I know . . . but I think I'm changing. Hey, Pan. If we
hadn't gone snooping in the Retiring Room, do you think
any of this would have happened?

PANTALAIMON. Not in *this* world. But there could be
another world where your father drank the poison . . .

LYRA. Yeah . . . or where the gyptians never found me . . .

PANTALAIMON. . . . or the Gobblers cut us apart . . .

LYRA. . . . or where Roger's alive.

SERAFINA *appears.*

SERAFINA. Lyra!

LYRA. Serafina Pekkala! What are you doing here?

SERAFINA. We've been searching for you throughout this
world.

LYRA *indicates the sleeping* WILL.

LYRA. Don't wake him!

SERAFINA. Who is this boy?

LYRA. It's Will. He's sick. He had two of his fingers cut off
with a knife.

SERAFINA. That must be the reason that I could come to
land. There are Spectres spread in a circle all around us, but
they'll come no nearer. They fear that knife.

She walks round WILL, *looking at him.*

He's a good-looking fellow, don't you think?

LYRA. Is he?

SERAFINA. There's some would think so. My sisters will be
here in a trice, so tell me quickly. What is he like?

LYRA. He's brave. He's good.

SERAFINA. Do you trust him?

LYRA. Yeah, I do . . . but why're you asking me all these
questions?

SERAFINA. It's hard for a witch to know what a short-lived
girl like you might feel for a boy. We live so long, you see,
for hundreds of years, never aging, never changing . . . and
men are quite the opposite. They're like butterflies, dead by
nightfall. We no sooner fall in love with them, than they're
gone. We bear their children, who are witches if they are
girls . . . but mortals like their fathers if they are boys . . .
and then we watch our sons growing strong and golden and
handsome, knowing all the time that they'll die of old age,
or on the battlefield, while we're still young, while we're
still bearing son after son, each one of them just as doomed
as the ones before. And finally our hearts are broken.

LYRA. Was Farder Coram in love with you?

Unseen by LYRA *or* SERAFINA, WILL *wakes and listens.*

SERAFINA. He was, and I loved him. I'd fallen to earth in the
Fenland marshes, where Coram was fishing, and he hauled
me into his boat, or I'd have drowned. He was twenty and
I was pushing two hundred . . . Well, I lay a week in his
cabin, with the light blocked out, while I was mending from
my fall. But it was summer outside, and the light was calling.
One afternoon we strolled across the fields. We picked fruits
from the hedgerows . . . we sat, we talked, we watched the
river . . . and I lifted a blackberry and pressed it against his
lips. It was only then, that I knew I loved him. Nine months
later, I bore his child . . .

LYRA. Was it a girl, a witch?

SERAFINA. He was a boy, and he died very young, in the
great fever. It tore a piece out of my heart, and Coram was
broken by it. I would have stayed and cared for him, but I
had to fly back to the North to be Queen of my clan. I hoped
that he would forget me, and find a human wife.

LYRA. He never did.

SERAFINA. I know that now. It seems that our destinies were bound together after all, like yours and this boy's may be.

WITCHES *appear.*

WITCHES. Serafina Pekkala! / We're here! / Have you found the child?

SERAFINA. Not so loud. There's a young man sleeping.

The WITCHES *look at* WILL *with great interest.*

We'll guard and guide these children wherever they wish to go. So tell us, Lyra, where are you heading for?

LYRA. We're looking for Will's dad. Only we don't know where to start.

KAISA. May I suggest that you ask the alethiometer?

LYRA. Will told me not to.

PANTALAIMON. But us and him are together, aren't we? Ask it where *we* oughta go. Then it won't be snooping.

LYRA. Well . . . just this once.

She silently asks the alethiometer.

We've got to travel to those blue mountains across the bay . . . and we gotta go fast. My mum's coming after me.

LORD ASRIEL'*s fortress.* LORD ASRIEL *addresses his troops.*

LORD ASRIEL. I stepped through the Aurora. I travelled through world after world, each one of them stranger and less familiar than the one before, until I'd found the limit that man can reach, a world beyond which lies only the spirit-domain of the Authority. And it's into this world, this final outpost of reality, that we shall tempt him. He will invade our world, and we shall fight him, just as the brightest and best beloved of all the angels fought him at the dawn of time. But with one difference. There is a knife, Æsahættr, celebrated in the Norsk legends, seen by Gilgamesh in a dream, foretold by the Delphic oracle to Alexander the Great. A knife so sharp, so keenly-edged that it can pierce his heart as though it were human flesh. We shall have that knife. We shall defeat the Authority. We shall topple him from his throne. We shall destroy him.

Applause.

STELMARIA. Fine words.

LORD ASRIEL. Be quiet.

STELMARIA. Why did you boast about the knife? You haven't got it.

LORD ASRIEL. Jopari will bring it. He's a man of honour.

STELMARIA. Jopari can't bring you anything. He's dying.

LORD ASRIEL. Then how can I get it?

STELMARIA. The Church has need of the knife as much as you, and they've got better intelligence. Send a spy to discover their plans.

LORD ASRIEL. I'll do it.

An OFFICER *appears, very amused.*

OFFICER. My Lord, your first recruit has arrived. But he's only that big!

He indicates minute size and the SOLDIERS *laugh.* LORD ASRIEL *signals to them to stop.*

LORD ASRIEL. Bring him to me and show him the greatest respect.

The OFFICER *goes.*

(*To the* OTHERS.) Lord Roke is here, the chief of the Gallivespians. I've seen him leading his men full-tilt against a Tartar battalion. He may be small, but he's a hero.

LORD ROKE *appears, flying on a dragonfly.*

LORD ROKE. Hello, chaps! I wouldn't have missed this party for the world!

He lands.

LORD ASRIEL. Lord Roke, what excellent timing.

LORD ROKE. A stirring speech, My Lord. We Gallivespians are right behind you. How can I be of service?

LORD ASRIEL. Since time immemorial, Lord Roke, your countrymen have crept through keyholes, hidden in cupboards, lurked in the pockets of coats to discover the secrets that we blundering humans cannot find out.

LORD ROKE. Are these kind remarks the prelude to some risky assignment?

LORD ASRIEL. They are. Won't you perch on my hand?

LORD ROKE. A singular honour. Pray take the greatest care to avoid my sting.

He sits on LORD ASRIEL's *hand.*

LORD ASRIEL. I want you to send your two most trusted spies to the Consistorial Court of Discipline in Geneva. They will report to me daily by lodestone resonator.

LORD ROKE. May I suggest the Chevalier Tialys and his spouse, the Lady Salmakia? Their sting is overwhelming, and they play very well as a team.

LORD ASRIEL. Whoever you wish. I want every detail, every hint of information they can provide about the god-destroying knife. I want to know where it is kept and how the Church is planning to capture it.

LORD ROKE. What a jaunt! And how they'll jump at it! I only wish it was me. I've also heard, Your Lordship . . .

He clears his throat significantly and beckons LORD ASRIEL *closer.*

. . . that the President of the Consistorial Court considers your daughter to be some kind of serious menace. Do you wish to know more about that?

LORD ASRIEL. She's of less importance.

STELMARIA. But be sure that your spies include her in their reports.

LORD ROKE. Mission understood!

He salutes and flies off.

Cittàgazze. The Torre degli Angeli. MRS COULTER *addresses the* SPECTRES, *with the* GOLDEN MONKEY *beside her.*

MRS COULTER. Spectres! Do you remember our bargain? I'll bring you human souls, and in return you'll leave us alone? Well, look what I've brought you. He's all yours! Aren't you hungry?

LORD BOREAL *drags* GIACOMO PARADISI *out of the door. Both are terrified.* PARADISI *looks in horror as the* SPECTRES *approach him.* CHILDREN, *including* PAOLO *and* ANGELICA, *appear and watch with unhealthy interest.* PARADISI *flails his hands in the air. Then his movements slow down and stop. He stands, lifeless and frozen.* MRS COULTER *inspects him, while the children pick his pockets.*

Total removal of the soul, just like Bolvangar. Stop whimpering, Charles! They've gone.

LORD BOREAL. Never, ever, put me through anything like this again.

MRS COULTER. We're in no danger! The Spectres and I have reached an understanding. As soon as you described them to me, I knew that I could dominate them, and so it turns out. Children, stay. This gentleman has a question for you. (*To* LORD BOREAL.) Go on!

LORD BOREAL. My dears, we're looking for a boy and a girl of about your age. Have you seen them?

PAOLO. Yeah.

ANGELICA. They're vile.

PAOLO. They're evil.

LORD BOREAL. Did the boy have a knife, when you saw him last?

ANGELICA. Yeah, he stole it from our brother Tullio.

PAOLO. Then Tullio got eaten by the Spectres, just like this old geezer.

ANGELICA. Except we wasn't laughing that time.

MRS COULTER. No, I'm sure you weren't. Where did they go, this boy and girl?

PAOLO. Up to the mountains, there, with lots of flying ladies.

ANGELICA. When you find the kids, will you kill 'em for us?

PAOLO. *Please!*

MRS COULTER. Carry our bags until we're out of the city, and we might consider it. And if you're really good, I'll give you a present. Do you like chocolatl?

They go.

Cittàgazze. In the mountains. Evening. The WITCHES, LYRA, WILL *and* PANTALAIMON *are on trek.* WILL *is nursing his hand. It's cold and they're all wrapped up.* SERAFINA *gives out orders.*

SERAFINA. Stop! This is where we'll rest for the night. Four of you stay in the air to keep a lookout.

GRIMHILD. What for?

CAITLIN. The Spectres won't come near us, not while the knife's about.

SERAFINA. There may be other dangers. You there, make a fire. You and you, get busy skinning our supper.

The WITCHES *get busy. Thunder.* SERAFINA *looks up at the sky.*

It's going to rain.

LYRA. Come on, Will. We'll all snuggle up together.

He sits with her.

WILL. Here, Pan! You're getting left out.

He lifts a corner of blanket next to him for PANTALAIMON, *who pointedly goes the long way round to* LYRA's *side and gets in with her.*

(*With irony.*) That's nice.

LYRA. He's never gonna touch you, Will. That's one of the rules.

WILL. I wish I had a daemon.

PANTALAIMON. You *have*.

LYRA. He's right. We're both human, en't we? It wouldn't make sense if you didn't have one.

WILL. Then why can't I see it?

LYRA. Not *it*. You can't see *her*, because *she* is inside you.

WILL. So there's daemons in my world?

LYRA. Yup.

WILL. It could be true. 'Cause I think there's Spectres there as well.

LYRA. What makes you think that?

WILL. Well . . . you remember what Tullio did, when the Spectres got him?

LYRA. Yeah, he got sorta interested in little tiny things, like the stones in the wall. What about it?

WILL. My mum does that. I haven't told you much about her. I've not told anyone, really. She gets ill, like ill in her head, with worry and fear. She'll count the railings in the park, or the leaves on a bush or the tins in a supermarket. As though she's turning away from something that frightens her. There's plenty of real things for her to be frightened of. My father never coming back, or the men who were after his letters. But it's more than that. It's things that nobody else can see. Maybe they're the same as Spectres, only in my world we call them something else. Like mad, or looney.

LYRA. Did you always want to find your dad?

WILL. Yeah, always. I used to pretend he was a prisoner in a dungeon, and I'd help him escape. Or a castaway on a desert island, and I'd be the captain of the boat that rescued him. I imagined him saying, 'Well done, my son.' No one on earth could have done better. I'm proud of you. My mother used to say I was gonna wear his mantle.

LYRA. What's a mantle?

WILL. It's a task, a purpose. But I could never wear my father's in a million years. He was a soldier, a fighter.

LYRA. You fought Tullio.

WILL. I had to, didn't I? Don't think I liked it.

LYRA. When I was at Jordan, I used to fight all the time, and I never been so happy in all my life. Did you not fight ever?

WILL. Just once. It was one of my mum's bad times. She went out of the house not properly dressed. Well, hardly dressed. There were some boys from school got hold of her, and they tormented her. Tortured her mentally. So the next day at school I found the boy who'd started it all. I broke his arm and I knocked out some of his teeth. Then afterwards I had to pretend I was sorry. The other kids all shut up about it. They knew that I'd kill them if they said anything that meant I got put into care, or my mum got taken away. After that, I lived a normal life. Had a couple of friends, even. But I never trusted kids again. They're just as keen as grown-ups to do bad things.

RUTA SKADI *appears.*

RUTA SKADI. Sisters! Take cover! There's a storm approaching!

WITCHES. Ruta Skadi! Welcome! Where have you been?

They welcome her to ground noisily.

RUTA SKADI. I flew to Lord Asriel's fortress. Oh, if you could see it, sisters! There are great stone ramparts and battlements and towers reaching up to the stars!

WITCHES. How did he build it so fast?

RUTA SKADI. Who knows? I think he makes time go faster or slower however he wants. And there are fighters joining him . . . humans, lizards and apes, huge birds with poisonous spurs . . . and witches from all the worlds! *Men*-witches too!

WITCHES. Never! / You're making it up!

SERAFINA. Did you see Lord Asriel?

RUTA SKADI. I did. I made myself invisible, and I found my way to his innermost chamber, while he was getting ready for sleep. And he asked us to join him. To fight on his side. Wouldn't you rather *that*, than sit on your arses skinning rabbits? Come with me! Fly to the battlefield!

There's a chorus of agreement from the WITCHES.

GRENDELLA. I will!

CAITLIN. I'll come too!

GRIMHILD. Can't we go there, Serafina Pekkala?

SERAFINA. No we can't, and you all know why! Let me talk to our sister.

SERAFINA *and* RUTA SKADI *talk where they can't be overheard.*

The prophecy's coming true. We've found the girl, and she's travelling with a boy.

RUTA SKADI *sees* LYRA *and* WILL.

RUTA SKADI. Is that him beside her? What's his name?

SERAFINA. It's Will.

RUTA SKADI. Come closer, Will.

WILL *comes nearer. He looks weaker and very ill.*

RUTA SKADI (*to* SERAFINA). What's wrong with his hand?

SERAFINA. It's a spirit-wound. Our spells can't heal it. The plants and herbs are all quite different in this world. (*To* LYRA *and* WILL.) Go back to sleep.

They do.

RUTA SKADI. I've seen those eyes before.

SERAFINA. If you have, it's best for us all that you forget them.

PIPISTRELLE *calls over, pointing upwards.*

PIPISTRELLE. Serafina Pekkala! There's a balloon being blown like a sea-bird through the skies!

WITCHES *look up and clamour.* RUTA SKADI *looks up with growing emotion.*

WITCHES. Who's inside it? / Is it him?

GRIMHILD. It's Jopari! It's Jopari with the Texan.

RUTA SKADI *turns furiously to* SERAFINA.

RUTA SKADI. Why did you bring Jopari into this world? Why didn't you stay in the Arctic, where you could do no harm?

SERAFINA. Don't make me angry, Ruta Skadi. All I have cared about, since that child came into our lives, is that the prophecy comes true.

RUTA SKADI. Then *let* it. Let it come true, or let it fail, if that's what destiny chooses. Lyra must do what she does of her own free will. Leave her alone!

Cittàgazze. MRS COULTER*'s camp.* MRS COULTER *and* LORD BOREAL. *He still has his gun. He's uneasy. She looks up and listens.*

MRS COULTER. When the thunder stops, I can hear the singing of the witches. Aren't you excited?

LORD BOREAL. I must confess, Marisa, that what's mostly absorbing my attention is the sight of those Spectres hovering in that copse of trees.

MRS COULTER. Yes, I'll have to find someone to give them soon. It's just a shame those ghastly children weren't a little bit older. I've been thinking, Charles, what a very good team we are. You needed me to stay alive . . .

LORD BOREAL. . . . and you needed me to guide you to your daughter.

MRS COULTER (*quietly to her* GOLDEN MONKEY). Though *that* particular task has been accomplished.

The GOLDEN MONKEY *signals approval.*

LORD BOREAL. What did you say?

MRS COULTER. Oh, nothing. What will you do, when we find the children?

LORD BOREAL. I'll get the knife, and hurry back to Geneva as fast as my legs will take me. What about you?

MRS COULTER. I'll keep my daughter quiet and safe. That's all I want. When she lived with me in London, I used to sit at the end of her bed and watch her, and my heart would burst with love. Then she'd wake up and . . . oh . . . the racketing round and the noise and nuisance. I'd have to remind myself of what she was like before, and then I'd love her again. What's odd is that I still don't know the most important thing about her.

LORD BOREAL. What might that be?

MRS COULTER. Remember the witch I tortured? 'It is the name of one who came before . . . ' What is that name?

LORD BOREAL. I've no idea.

MRS COULTER. Don't treat me like a fool. I'm sure the Church has worked it out by now. I'm certain they've told you.

LORD BOREAL. Marisa, they haven't!

MRS COULTER. I'm warning you, Charles! Unless you tell me *now*, you will die a revolting death. And I can do it! (*She calls.*) Spectres! Come closer!

SPECTRES *approach as* LORD BOREAL *quakes in terror. The* GOLDEN MONKEY, *terrified, scuttles over to* MRS COULTER *and hides behind her.*

LORD BOREAL. Marisa, I promise . . . I swear . . . I do not know that name. Don't you believe me?

She looks at him and forms a judgement.

MRS COULTER. Yes, I believe you. And I'm sorry to say that it makes you utterly useless to me. Spectres! Take him!

The SPECTRES *attack and devour him.*

(*To the* GOLDEN MONKEY.) Let's go.

The WITCHES*' camp. Moonlight. The* WITCHES *are sleeping.* LYRA *and* WILL *are lying on the ground.* SERAFINA *approaches.*

SERAFINA. Pantalaimon!

PANTALAIMON. Ssh! Lyra's asleep.

SERAFINA. I must go. Ruta Skadi has left in a rage, and I'm terrified of what she might do.

KAISA. Tell Will to get some sleep as well.

They go.

WILL. Sleep! That's the last thing I could do. Look at my hand.

He shows his hand, which is septic and gangrenous.

It's worse than ever. I never knew anything could hurt so much. The blood's gushing out of it, and it's bad, it's smelling. Am I going to die? I'm so frightened.

PANTALAIMON *licks his hand.*

What are you doing?

PANTALAIMON. Lyra doesn't think you're frightened. She thinks you're the bravest fighter she's ever seen. She thinks you're as brave as Iorek Byrnison.

LYRA *opens her eyes and listens.*

WILL. She's braver than me. She's the best friend I ever had.

PANTALAIMON. She thinks that about you as well.

WILL. What would she think of me if I died like this? In the middle of nowhere . . . on a stupid search for a father who went through a window and vanished . . .

PANTALAIMON. He's still alive.

WILL. He didn't bother to come home, though, did he? I've been lying here trying to think what to do. But the pain's so bad, and I get so muddled.

He stands.

I'm going for a walk.

He goes. LYRA *sits up.*

LYRA. You touched him.

PANTALAIMON. I felt sorry for him.

LYRA. Shall I go after him?

PANTALAIMON. No, don't. He wants to be on his own.

LYRA. He said I was the best friend he ever had. What if that's the last thing I ever hear him say?

PANTALAIMON. It'll be the last thing and the best.

LYRA. Yeah. Yeah, you're right.

The GOLDEN MONKEY *appears and creeps towards her.* MRS COULTER *appears.* LYRA *sees it and springs up.*

MRS COULTER. Lyra! Lyra, it's me.

LYRA. Go away!

MRS COULTER. Don't be afraid. I'm taking you back to our own world, darling, to our beautiful world of daemons. Come to your mother.

LYRA. Will! Will!

The WITCHES *awake and see* MRS COULTER.

WITCHES. It's her! / The woman with the monkey daemon! / The torturing-woman!

MRS COULTER. Spectres! Now for the feast!

SPECTRES attack the WITCHES, *who shudder and struggle as their souls are devoured.* LYRA *screams for help.* MRS COULTER *and the* GOLDEN MONKEY *carry her away.*

Cittàgazze. On the mountain. There's a rock in the shape of an eagle. WILL *appears, in great pain.* JOPARI *appears out of the darkness.*

JOPARI. Give me your hand.

WILL stares at him.

WILL. Who are you?

JOPARI. It doesn't matter. Give it to me.

Cautiously, WILL *holds out his hand.* JOPARI *takes out a little flask and puts ointment on it.*

I came to this world to look for an old, old man. And he sent me to you . . . and I discover you're just a child. Well, so it must be. Don't move.

He has finished anointing WILL's *hand.*

There.

WILL. It's stopped hurting. Even the bleeding's stopped.

JOPARI. Have you got the knife?

WILL. What . . . ?

JOPARI. Let me see it.

WILL. Here.

He gives it to JOPARI, *who looks at it.*

JOPARI. Do you know who made this?

WILL. No.

JOPARI. It was invented by the philosophers of Cittàgazze, three hundred years ago. They wanted to divide matter . . .

to cut it smaller and smaller, till they'd made a particle so
minute that even the strongest lens couldn't detect it . . . and
then to divide that too. This was the result. It worked. It
worked triumphantly. But they'd unleashed a power they
couldn't control. The knife cut windows into other worlds,
and the Spectres floated in. Here, take it.

WILL. I don't want it.

JOPARI. Too late. You think you chose this knife. Or that you
stumbled across it. Wrong. It chose you. You are the Bearer.
If you don't use it now to fight the forces of evil, it will be
torn from you and used against the rest of the human race,
for all eternity.

WILL. Forget it, will you? I'm not gonna fight. I hate fighting.

JOPARI. Did you fight to get it?

WILL. Yes.

JOPARI. And did you win it in single combat?

WILL. Yes.

JOPARI. Then you're a fighter. You're a warrior. Argue with
me if you like, but don't argue against your own nature.
Now listen. There are two great powers, and they've been
enemies ever since time began. There's the power that wants
us to obey and be humble and submit, and the power that
wants us to know more, and be wiser and stronger. Every
advance in human life, every scrap of knowledge and
wisdom and decency has been torn by one side from the
teeth of the other. Now those two powers are lining up in
battle. Each of them needs that knife. You have to choose.
We've both been guided to this place, this night, this
moment . . . you with the knife, and me to tell you what
you must do with it.

WILL. You're wrong! I know what I'm doing. I'm searching,
right? And it's not for the knife. It's . . .

JOPARI. Your search is over. You found what you were *meant*
to find. Now you must take it to Lord Asriel. Tell him that
this is the weapon he needs above all others, Æsahættr. Set

off at once. Ignore everything else, no matter how important it may seem. Guides will show you the way. The night is full of angels.

WILL *moves away.*

Wait. I'll never meet you again. I'm dying. Let me see what you look like.

He strikes a match. They stare at each other.

You're my son. You're Will.

An arrow strikes him, and he falls dead.

WILL. Father?

RUTA SKADI *appears, bow and arrow in hand.*

RUTA SKADI. Jopari!

WILL. What have you done? I looked for him all my life, and now you've killed him. Why?

RUTA SKADI. I loved him. And he rejected me, for the sake of your mother and you! I am a witch! I don't forgive! I can't forgive! Yambe-Akka, take me!

She stabs herself and dies. WILL *goes to his* FATHER.

WILL. Father . . . Dad, Daddy . . . Father. You loved us. I'm sorry I doubted you. I'll do what you want, I swear it. I'll be the man that you want me to be. I'll fight. I'll be a warrior. I'll take this knife to Lord Asriel, wherever he is.

In the far distance, LYRA *can be heard calling.*

LYRA. Will! Help me! She's taking me away!

WILL. Lyra?

He runs back to the WITCHES' *camp. The* WITCHES *are standing dead and frozen.*

WILL. Lyra! Lyra!

He finds the place where he and LYRA *were sleeping.*

Oh God. Oh God. She's gone.

SERAFINA *and* KAISA *are there.*

SERAFINA. It was the woman with the monkey daemon. She killed my witches.

KAISA. All of them, all of them.

WILL. Where's Lyra?

SERAFINA. Her mother has taken her, Will. I arrived too late. Where were you?

WILL. I found my father. And now he's dead. But he gave me a task. I've got to take this knife to Lord Asriel.

SERAFINA. So the choice is yours. Either save the world, or save your friend. I know which I would do . . .

KAISA *stops her continuing.*

But I can't help you to decide. Ruta Skadi was right. I meddled in human lives, and brought destruction on my sisters. If all goes well for you and Lyra, we'll meet on the battlefield. Farewell.

She goes. WILL *picks up* LYRA*'s rucksack. He takes out the alethiometer and looks at it.*

WILL. Which should I choose?

Two angels, BALTHAMOS *and* BARUCH, *appear.*

Who are you?

BALTHAMOS. We are angels. We have been following your father. We hoped he would lead us to you . . .

BARUCH. . . . and he did.

WILL. Why didn't you save him?

BARUCH. We protected him all the time until he found you.

BALTHAMOS. Then his task was over. Now we must lead you to Lord Asriel.

WILL *hesitates.*

What are you waiting for?

WILL. I'll do that later.

He holds out the alethiometer.

I want you to help me find the girl that this belongs to.

BARUCH. Have you forgotten your father's orders?

BATHAMOS. You must ignore everything else, never mind how important it might seem.

WILL. Are you stronger than me, or weaker?

BALTHAMOS. Weaker. You've got flesh. We're only made of spirit.

WILL. Right, then I'm telling you. Help me to find her.

BALTHAMOS. Ask us politely and we may.

WILL. Do you know where her mother's taken her?

BARUCH. We know where she came from.

BALTHAMOS. From a tent nearby with a dead man eaten by Spectres.

WILL. What does he look like?

BARUCH. Pasty. Silvery hair. Sixty.

WILL. She's killed Lord Boreal. That's something good. One of you follow her, fast as you can. Come back and tell me where they've gone. The other one stay.

BARUCH. You are making a great mistake . . .

BALTHAMOS. . . . but we have no choice.

A cave. Red silk prayer-scarves, a waterfall, a rainbow. LYRA *is asleep.* ROGER*'s ghost appears.*

ROGER. Lyra? Can you hear me?

LYRA *stirs in her sleep, then half wakes up.*

LYRA. Rodge, where are you?

ROGER. Help me, Lyra. I'm in a terrible place. It's grey, all grey. No hope, no nothing. Come to me, Lyra. Won't you rescue me?

LYRA. Rodge!

MRS COULTER *comes in, carrying a bowl containing a sleeping draught. She hurries to* LYRA *and feeds her with a spoon.*

MRS COULTER. Don't be upset, my darling, it's only a dream. I've brought your medicine. It will keep you calm, it'll keep you sleeping.

ROGER *disappears as* LYRA *sleeps more deeply.*

How lovely you look. Are you happy like this? I am.

Cittàgazze. MRS COULTER*'s camp.* WILL *is putting things in a bag.* LORD BOREAL *is standing dead, as when last seen.* BALTHAMOS *is there.*

WILL. Do you think I need anything else?

BALTHAMOS. You need some inner resource to help you recognise my age-old wisdom and respect it.

WILL. What's the matter? You hungry or something?

BALTHAMOS. Angels don't get hungry.

WILL. So you don't want any of this?

BALTHAMOS. What is it?

WILL. Kendal Mint Cake.

BALTHAMOS. I might try a little out of interest.

WILL *gives him some, and* BALTHAMOS *nibbles it fastidiously.*

WILL. Have you and your friend got names?

BALTHAMOS. I am Balthamos, and my friend is Baruch.

WILL. Who sent you?

BALTHAMOS. We sent ourselves. We heard the rumour of
Lord Asriel's war, and it inspired us to join him. But we
wanted to take him something more, because we're not
high-ranking in the heavenly scheme of things. We wanted
to bring the knife. To see the Authority killed, and his
Clouded Mountain laid to waste, is an ambition that Baruch
and I have nursed for many centuries.

WILL. Have you always been angels?

BALTHAMOS. I was created in my present form. Baruch used
to be a man.

WILL. When?

BALTHAMOS. Only four thousand years ago. I date from the
antediluvian era, but the difference in our age is not
important.

WILL. So do people become angels when they die?

BALTHAMOS. Mostly not. May I ask the point of this
metaphysical speculation?

WILL. My father's just died, that's the point. What mostly
happens when people die?

BALTHAMOS. They go to the world of the dead.

WILL. What's it like?

BALTHAMOS. It's a prison camp. That's all we know. That's
all that anyone knows. The Church tells people that, if
they're good, they'll go to heaven. But that's a lie.

WILL. He's in a prison camp?

BALTHAMOS. Of course, like the countless millions who
died before him. Now that you've loaded up the dead man's
property, can we move on? Baruch will be here in a matter
of seconds.

WILL. How do you know? Do you read his mind?

BALTHAMOS. I'm *in* his mind, and he is in mine.

BARUCH appears.

BARUCH. Balthamos!

BALTHAMOS. My heart, my own!

They embrace and hold hands.

Well?

BARUCH. Lyra is in the world she came from, in a cave
  beneath a range of snowy mountains. I've drawn it for Will.

He produces a map. WILL looks at it.

There's a waterfall where the ice and mist form rainbows.
Red silk banners fly in the wind. The woman with the
monkey daemon is keeping her asleep.

WILL. What with?

BARUCH. A potion. Lyra has not been harmed. She's
  dreaming.

WILL. Good, so I won't need you two.

BALTHAMOS. You'll need us to find Lord Asriel.

WILL. No I won't, because Lyra can read the alethiometer. All
  right?

BALTHAMOS. No, not all right. How do we know you'll go
  to Lord Asriel? You've already delayed it once.

WILL. Do you think I'm just gonna ignore my father, after
  what happened? You're not human.

BARUCH. Obviously.

BALTHAMOS. The notion of having a father at all is quite
  incomprehensible to the average angel.

BARUCH. Let's compromise. I'll fly on, and tell Lord Asriel
  that you're on your way . . .

BALTHAMOS. . . . and I shall remain with Will.

WILL. I don't need *either* of you.

BALTHAMOS. You do. In Lyra's world, you'll need a daemon or you'll look very much out of place. I can be one.

WILL. You mean, change into a bird or something?

BALTHAMOS. That is exactly what I mean. It will be unspeakably humiliating, and I'll do it only when it's absolutely essential. Wait over there.

WILL picks up his bags and goes. BALTHAMOS *addresses* BARUCH.

It was painful to be parted from you.

BARUCH. It was painful for me to be in a world of mortals. I remembered so clearly what it was like to be one myself. I longed for a body like they possess, so warm and sensuous. I envied them.

BALTHAMOS. Fly with care. Lord Asriel's fortress is surrounded by enemy angels. My heart goes with you.

They embrace. BARUCH *flies off.*

Oxford / Oxford. The Botanic Gardens. LYRA *and* WILL *are there.*

LYRA. I was frightened that I'd never wake up, that I'd be stuck in the place that I was dreaming about. There was mist all round me . . . grey mist and a grey sky, and an enormous grey plain, trodden flat by the people there. There were millions of them, young, old, pale, dark . . . all crammed together, all sad and sorrowful.

WILL. 'A prison camp.' The moment the angel said those words, everything changed.

LYRA. Then I saw Roger. He was the only one there with hope in his eyes. He called my name and he ran to me and I tried to throw my arms around him, but they went right through the air.

WILL. I could feel the words I wanted to say to my father
bursting inside me. I had to see him. Had to talk to him.
It was my task . . .

LYRA. I said, 'I'll find you, Rodge. I swore it before, and
I swear it again.'

WILL. . . . It was my mantle.

A message is seen / heard from LORD ROKE.

LORD ROKE. *Lord Roke attempting contact with our
Gallivespian agents in Geneva . . . testing, testing . . . come
in, Chevalier, are you hearing me . . . ?*

The Consistorial Court of Discipline. A corridor. BROTHER
JASPER *approaches the* PRESIDENT *at a run, practically
tripping over his soutane. He carries the alethiometer and
a handful of notes. Two Gallivespians, the* CHEVALIER
TIALYS *and* LADY SALMAKIA, *are seen eavesdropping.*

BROTHER JASPER. Father President! Forgive my haste. It's
the alethiometer. It's pouring out information!

PRESIDENT. What has it told you?

BROTHER JASPER. Lyra Belacqua is being kept a captive . . .
by her mother in . . . yes, in a cave in the mountains.
They've never yet been explored, so the alethiometer wasn't
able to give me a map-reference . . . but there's a rainbow
above the cave and a row of red silk flags, heathen flags,
they're a method of prayer.

PRESIDENT. Which world is Lyra in?

BROTHER JASPER. She's in our world. And so is the boy.

PRESIDENT. The *boy*?

BROTHER JASPER. That's what I came running to tell you.
There's a boy, the Bearer of the knife we spoke of. He's

Lyra's friend. He's *part of her story*. It seems the prophecy's moving even faster than we feared.

PRESIDENT. We must pray that we have enough time to counteract it. Have you assembled the band of brothers, as I told you?

BROTHER JASPER. I have.

PRESIDENT. Are they skilled in combat, staunch in belief and willing to lose their lives for the holy purpose?

BROTHER JASPER. They are, Father President. So am I.

PRESIDENT. Then it falls to you, Brother Jasper, to save us from the doom that threatens us all. Find out the precise location of the cave. Once you have done so, you and your holy brethren will approach it by zeppelin. What you must do there will be hard for you. Your whole nature will rise up in revolt. Subdue it. By killing the child before she can be tempted, you will save her soul. Kneel.

BROTHER JASPER *does. The* PRESIDENT *takes a medallion from around his neck and places it round* BROTHER JASPER*'s.*

This sacred medallion of Saint Martin Luther absolves the wearer from every crime, past and present. Wear it for Lyra. Come.

As he and BROTHER JASPER *leave, the* CHEVALIER TIALYS *and* LADY SALMAKIA *relay a message on their lodestone resonator. We cross-fade to* LORD ASRIEL's *fortress: the war room.* AIDES *and* OFFICERS *are studying maps, plotting battle positions, etc.* LORD ASRIEL *and* LORD ROKE *see the* CHEVALIER TIALYS's *message as it appears.*

TIALYS. . . . . *Your loyal spies present their compliments from Geneva . . . the Church's alethiometer is now dangerously effective thanks to skilful reader . . .*

LORD ASRIEL. And?

TIALYS. . . . *a boy has taken the knife from Cittàgazze, into the daemon-world . . .*

LORD ASRIEL. To where exactly?

TIALYS. . . . *news of your daughter, however, is more abundant . . .*

LORD ASRIEL. Lord Roke, are these spies of yours any good?

LORD ROKE. They are Gallivespians of ancient lineage, My Lord. I hope you do not equate small size with small ability.

SALMAKIA. . . . *Lyra is in a cave in the Northern mountains . . . her mother is keeping her in a trance . . .*

LORD ASRIEL. Her mother? Stuck in a cave? I don't believe it. This is a woman who has her hair done twice a week at six in the morning.

TIALYS. . . . *the Church will send a band of assassins to the cave by zeppelin. Their orders will be to eliminate Lyra without delay. Transmission over.*

LORD ASRIEL. Eliminate Lyra? Why? She's not important. She's just a foul-mouthed brat with grubby fingernails. Why are they trying to kill her?

STELMARIA. You'd have killed her yourself, at Svalbard.

LORD ASRIEL. No, I would not! I thought I'd *have* to kill her, for the sake of my experiment. When the boy walked in, I was vastly relieved and I let her go. But I can't help wondering now if that was a fatal error. Should I have kept her with me? Should I have brought her here?

An OFFICER *bursts in.*

OFFICER. My Lord! An angel has arrived! An angel to join your army.

All in the room are jubilant. BARUCH *appears, badly wounded. The* SOLDIERS *present are awe-struck: this is the first angel any of them have seen.*

BARUCH. Greetings, Lord Asriel.

LORD ASRIEL. You're wounded!

BARUCH. I was attacked by enemy angels on my way here. I will not live to fight for you. Others will come to you, they will flock in their millions. I'm just a messenger.

He stops to collect his strength. LORD ASRIEL *turns away.*

LORD ASRIEL. Well?

BARUCH. The knife . . . Æsahættr . . .

LORD ASRIEL *turns to look at him.*

LORD ASRIEL (*tense*). Do you know where it is?

BARUCH. Jopari has sent it to you. His warrior son will bring it . . .

LORD ASRIEL. When will he come?

BARUCH. I don't know. He disobeyed his father's orders . . . he's gone . . .

LORD ASRIEL. Where?

BARUCH. . . . he's gone to the cave where your daughter is held a prisoner. Bring me a map, I can show you . . .

Somebody does.

LORD ROKE. It's too late, My Lord. His light is fading.

BARUCH *points to a place on the map.*

LORD ASRIEL. No, he's pointing.

BARUCH. Oh, Balthamos!

He dies.

LORD ASRIEL. The paper is cold where his finger touched it. The cave is here. Lord Roke, order our spies in Geneva to conceal themselves in one of the Church's aircraft. They will brief you hourly on the enemy's plan of attack. And order six gyropters ready to take to the air at once.

LORD ROKE. Who will command them?

LORD ASRIEL. I shall. I'll fly to the cave. I'll capture the knife and save my daughter.

STELMARIA. So do you care about her?

LORD ASRIEL. Yes I do! It's like a chess game, when you suddenly realise that your opponent is concentrating all his energies on capturing some insignificant little piece to which you had never attached the remotest value. You don't know why he wants it. But if it matters to him, then it matters to you. You have to defend it.

LYRA*'s world. Snowy foothills.* WILL *and* BALTHAMOS *are travelling.*

BALTHAMOS. Baruch is dead! Baruch is dead!

He flies into the air.

WILL. Balthamos! Don't leave me! I need you!

But BALTHAMOS *has disappeared.* WILL *gets out a map and studies it.* BEARS *appear and approach him with hungry eyes.* WILL *turns and sees them.*

What do you want?

The BEARS *confer among themselves.*

1ST BEAR. What is it?

2ND BEAR. It's got no daemon.

3RD BEAR. Is it spirit or flesh?

The 1ST BEAR *touches* WILL.

1ST BEAR. It's flesh!

BEARS. It's meat! It's food! Food! Food!

WILL. Get back! I've got a knife!

BEARS. A knife!

They laugh derisively. IOREK *appears.*

IOREK. What's this?

1ST BEAR. It's a warm-blooded creature, Your Majesty. We don't know what it is, but we've not eaten for days. We're starving!

The BEARS *bellow with hunger.*

BEARS. Kill him! / We're hungry! / We want to eat!

WILL. You can't eat me! I'm a human being!

The BEARS *roar angrily.*

IOREK. That's the worst thing you could have said!

BEARS. We hate humans!

IOREK. It was a human woman who corrupted Svalbard! It was a human man who blew a hole in the sky and let the sun in! So why should you be spared, you shivering sprat, you pale-faced porpoise, you two-legged shrimp?

A chorus of agreement from the BEARS.

WILL. I'll show you. I challenge you to fight me in single combat.

The BEARS *roar with laughter.*

If I lose, you can kill me and eat me, whatever you like. But if I win . . . you've got to take me up to the mountains. You've got to stay with me, and fight for me whenever I tell you.

IOREK. I will not fight you! It would be shameful! You are as weak as an oyster out of its shell.

WILL. You're right! I am! It's not a fair contest at all. You've got all that armour, and I've got none. You could take off my head with one sweep of your paw. Make it fairer. Give me one piece of your armour, any bit you like. Then we'll be evenly matched, and there won't be any shame in fighting me.

IOREK. Take this.

With a snarl, he removes his helmet and throws it down at WILL's *feet.* WILL *picks it up and looks at it carefully.*

WILL. So this is your armour? It doesn't look very strong to me. Let me see.

He draws the knife and slices up the helmet. The BEARS *mutter in fear.*

Well, that was your armour. And this is my knife. And since your helmet wasn't any use to me, I'll have to fight you without it. Are you ready, bear? I think we're well matched. I could take off your head with one sweep of my knife, after all.

IOREK *steps back, and so do the other* BEARS.

IOREK. It is too strong a weapon. I can't fight it. Boy, you win.

The BEARS *growl in recognition.*

Now show it to me.

WILL. I will only show this knife to a bear I've heard about, who I know I can trust. He's the King of the bears, and a good friend of the girl I'm going to the mountains to look for. Her name is Lyra Silvertongue. The bear is called Iorek Byrnison.

IOREK. I am Iorek Byrnison.

WILL. I know you are.

He holds out the knife.

Here, hold it carefully.

He hands IOREK *the knife.* IOREK *looks at it.*

IOREK. This is the edge you cut my armour with. It's sharp enough.

He turns it over.

But *this* edge is the most fearful thing I've ever seen. I can't tell what it is, or how it was made. How did you come by it?

WILL. I won it in a fight. I'm taking it to use in a war on Lord Asriel's side. But first, I've got to rescue Lyra.

He unfolds the map.

She's being held a prisoner in a cave, and it's somewhere up that river and in these mountains.

IOREK. That's where we bears are travelling. We've lost our hunting grounds. The ocean is warm, the seals have died, the ice is melting. But I have heard that in those mountains, there are wild creatures aplenty and snows that last for ever. Come with us.

The BEARS *roar in approval.* BALTHAMOS *appears.*

BALTHAMOS. Forgive me, Will. I was disabled by my grief. But one must do what is right, even after you've lost the one you love.

IOREK. Who is this?

WILL. It's Balthamos. He's an angel. This is Iorek Byrnison, the King of the Svalbard bears.

IOREK. We've heard of angels. We see them as points of light in the Northern skies. But never before have I met one face to face.

BALTHAMOS. Nor I a bear.

IOREK. Let's go!

They go.

Geneva. The Consistorial Court of Discipline. BROTHER JASPER *addresses an assembly.*

BROTHER JASPER. Fellow-warriors of the Brotherhood of the Holy Purpose! I, your leader, will now confide in you our plan of action.

A map of LYRA's *world appears.*

First, the greater picture. This is our world. There at Svalbard is the huge connecting route that Lord Asriel blasted through into Cittàgazze . . . with the environmental consequences that we've seen . . . melting ice-caps, rising sea-levels, the opening-up of random windows too many to be displayed and a vast increase in the draining-away of Dust.

A map of Cittàgazze appears.

I'm showing the worlds side by side because it's clearer like this, although in life, of course, they occupy the identical space. Lyra followed Lord Asriel through here into Cittàgazze, while he moved on to the strange, anonymous, astral world in which he's built his fortress.

A map of our world appears. Other maps follow as needed.

There's a window *here* between Cittàgazze and a curious world that boasts a parallel Oxford, very like ours. Lord Boreal used to take this route before the Spectres arrived in such vast numbers, and so did Will and Lyra in their journeyings round the knife. *This* is a derelict Arctic gap, discovered twelve years ago by the shaman Jopari, who has thankfully now been killed. *This* is the window through which Mrs Coulter carried Lyra back to our world, and into the cave of rainbows. *That* is the cave!

He points it out.

Lord Asriel is leading a force of six gyropters through his Svalbard window, and they will shortly approach the cave from *here*. The boy with the knife was taken upriver by the King of the armoured bears, and they will arrive from *here*. We shall advance by zeppelin from *this* direction and arrive at the cave at the same time as our enemies. The battle will follow. The advantage is to us, because Lord Asriel will be trying to carry his daughter home alive, whereas our aim can be achieved with two strokes of the sword: one for the girl, and one for the boy. The second great prize, the knife, will then be ours. In brief, dear brothers in faith, dear holy pilgrims, you who will survive the battle with lifelong honour, you who will fall and rise to a blissful eternity, we depart on a sacred mission. We shall save Lyra Belacqua from the damnation of the witches' prophecy. We shall save the world!

Applause.

Near the cave. WILL, IOREK *and* BALTHAMOS *arrive, accompanied by other* BEARS.

IOREK. Listen!

They do.

Zeppelins are approaching from the South.

WILL. Ssh.

He listens.

What's that?

IOREK. Gyropters from the North. We must rescue Lyra now, before they attack.

BALTHAMOS. The cave is there.

WILL. Right, this is what we'll do. I'll go to the cave. I'll wait till it's empty. Then I'll wake up Lyra . . .

BALTHAMOS. A great mistake!

WILL. I've done it before, all right? I'll cut a window, then I'll bring her back through a different world . . .

BALTHAMOS. Her mother might find you.

WILL. What if she does? She can't do anything.

BALTHAMOS. She can do much.

IOREK. She will enchant you, like she enchanted Iofur Raknison.

WILL. Me? Get enchanted by her? Yes, that's *really* likely, after she kidnapped Lyra, and slagged me off to that poncey pal of hers . . . and then she *killed* him! I'm not going to hang about, you can be sure of that. Just keep an eye out for the monkey.

He walks to the cave and goes in. LYRA *is there, asleep.*

Lyra? Lyra! Sit up.

She remains asleep. He eases her up.

That's right. Come on. I'm cutting us out.

With one arm around LYRA, *he reaches out with the knife to cut a window.* MRS COULTER *appears at the mouth of the cave, with her bowl of medicine.*

MRS COULTER. Will! Thank God you're here.

WILL. How did you know who I am?

MRS COULTER. Who else would be so brave as to come at a time like this? We've not a moment to lose. Quick, cut a window into another world, and we'll all go through.

WILL. All?

MRS COULTER. Yes, all. Lyra, you and me.

WILL. Stay where you are! I'm rescuing her, not you.

MRS COULTER. Why not?

WILL. Because she wouldn't want you anywhere near her. She hates you. Didn't you know that? Keep away!

He holds out the knife, ready to cut a window.

MRS COULTER. Is that the knife?

WILL. Yeah, ten out of ten.

MRS COULTER. Let me look at it.

WILL. No! Be quiet!

MRS COULTER. Why?

WILL. Because the knife could break if . . .

MRS COULTER. What?

WILL. Nothing.

MRS COULTER. Do you mean, if you were distracted?

WILL. Forget I said it. Lyra. Lyra, stand up. We're going.

MRS COULTER. Take me too.

WILL. No! You've got a nerve even to ask, when it was you that kidnapped Lyra and made her a prisoner.

MRS COULTER. I had to. She's in danger from the Church.

WILL. She knows that! She's escaped them over and over
again. She didn't need any help from you. She never asked
you to turn her into a pet, a zombie! Look, I'm not arguing,
right? 'Cause that's exactly what you want. Keep away.

*He prepares once again to cut a window, but has difficulty
concentrating.*

MRS COULTER. You're right, she hates me. Even after all the
sacrifices I've made for her. I've had to cut myself off from
the Church, the Church that has comforted and supported
me all my life. But I must protect my daughter. And if that
means keeping her fast asleep, so be it. Wouldn't *your*
mother do the same for you? Wouldn't she, Will?

WILL *turns to her.*

WILL. You don't know anything about my mother.

MRS COULTER. I'm sure she looks after you.

WILL *is angry and upset.*

WILL. I look after her, as it happens. Shut up about her.

Aircraft are directly overhead.

MRS COULTER. They're here. Cut the window. Cut it and let
us all through. Now!

Gunfire and sounds of approaching battle.

WILL. Stand back! I'm taking Lyra!

MRS COULTER *produces a revolver and aims it at* WILL.

MRS COULTER. Stay where you are! I'm holding you captive!

The CHEVALIER TIALYS *and* LADY SALMAKIA
appear beside her.

WILL. What, as hostages?

MRS COULTER. Yes, hostages! They all want the knife and
they all want Lyra! You're my only chance!   ·

The GALLIVESPIANS *sting her ankle. She screams and
falls to the ground.*

I've been stung! It's agony!

She sees the GALLIVESPIANS.

What are those *things*?

LYRA *starts to wake.*

LYRA. What's happening? Where are we?

WILL. You've been asleep. Come on. Get up.

He poises the knife.

LYRA. Oh Will, I had an amazing dream.

WILL. Don't talk. We're getting out. Hold on to me tight.

He tries to find a snag in the air. The cave is invaded by
BROTHERS OF THE HOLY PURPOSE. *They advance on*
LYRA *and* WILL. MRS COULTER *fires at them, from her*
place on the ground. LORD ASRIEL *appears, with a troop*
of his SOLDIERS.

MRS COULTER. Asriel!

LORD ASRIEL. Lyra!

LYRA. No! Go away!

LORD ASRIEL *and his soldiers attack the* BROTHERS.
Meanwhile:

It's him! It's my dad! Cut a window, quick!

WILL *stands poised to do so, trying to concentrate.*

MRS COULTER. Lyra, don't go!

WILL. Don't talk to her.

MRS COULTER. My precious, my dear one. Help me!

WILL. Quiet!

MRS COULTER. Lyra, don't leave me here to die.

WILL. Tell her to shut up. If I don't concentrate, the knife's
gonna break.

LORD ASRIEL *breaks from the fighting and addresses*
WILL.

LORD ASRIEL. Will! Give me the knife!

LYRA. Don't listen to him! Cut a window!

LORD ASRIEL. Give it to me!

LYRA. Go away! Cut a window! Will!

WILL. I'm trying.

He tries with all his might to concentrate.

LORD ASRIEL. Will! Do as your father told you! Think of your father! *Think of your father!*

WILL. Dad?

The knife shatters. More BROTHERS *invade the cave.* LORD ASRIEL *fights them off while protecting* LYRA. BALTHAMOS *is seen fleeing in a panic. Under cover of the fighting,* WILL *picks up the pieces of the knife and pulls* LYRA *away and out of the cave.* LORD ASRIEL *looks around and sees that she has gone.*

LORD ASRIEL. Lyra! Lyra!

End of Act One.

ACT TWO

LORD ASRIEL's *fortress.* LORD ASRIEL, *alone.*

LORD ASRIEL. I dreamt last night of the angel who
challenged the Authority all those aeons ago. The angel who
failed because the knife that could deliver the death-blow
hadn't yet been invented. I was falling with him down an
endless abyss, into a blackness so intense that it seemed
to invade my brain. But I could feel the rush of his wings
beside me, and I asked him . . . did he know, had he
suspected . . . that from this night on, he would be held
responsible for everything bad that ever happened . . .
every temptation, every atrocity, every crime? He laughed.
He said he wasn't surprised at all. He knew the system.
The recording angels always put the blame on the losing
side. And then I woke, and remembered that the knife was
broken.

LORD ASRIEL's *fortress. The war room. Aides and officers
pause in their work to watch the latest dispatch from the*
CHEVALIER TIALYS *and* LADY SALMAKIA. LORD
ASRIEL *listens, his hand on* STELMARIA. LORD ROKE
operates the receiving-equipment.

TIALYS. . . . *The Chevalier Tialys and Lady Salmakia report
from the site of the recent battle.*

LORD ASRIEL. Have they found my daughter?

TIALYS. *Our tour of the surroundings reveals heavy losses by
the enemy . . .*

SALMAKIA. . . . *young men in clerical garb who had adopted
near-suicidal tactics.*

LORD ASRIEL. But why?

SALMAKIA. *On the body of one, we found these battle orders . . .*

She holds up a piece of paper.

. . . of which the final sentence is of interest . . .

She reads it out.

. . . 'We shall save Lyra Belacqua from the damnation of the witches' prophecy. We shall save the world!'

LORD ASRIEL. A prophecy? I was right. She *is* important. But where is she now?

LORD ROKE. I think we're coming to that, My Lord.

TIALYS. *Lyra and the boy emerged from their hiding-place after the close of fighting. We are observing them, and will shortly bring them to Your Lordship's fortress by gyropter.*

The GALLIVESPIANS' *image fades.*

LORD ASRIEL. She'll soon be here.

STELMARIA. Don't be too sure.

LORD ROKE. I'd like to echo your daemon's doubts, My Lord. It's the absence of the knife that worries me most. Even the broken pieces would be better than nothing. I wonder why Your Lordship didn't collect them?

LORD ASRIEL. What, scrabble in the dirt to pick them up? I wouldn't demean the knife like that. I wouldn't demean myself, or the boy either. He'll bring me the useless remains when the time is right, and on his own terms. That's how it must be.

LORD ROKE. A sentiment after my own heart, My Lord! We Gallivespians have few victories to our name but, by golly, we lose with honour!

LYRA*'s world. Near the cave.* LYRA *and* WILL *are there.*

LYRA. You mean, your father was Jopari?

WILL. Yeah, that's right! And he gave me the knife and he told me to take it to Lord Asriel. But I put that off for a bit so I could rescue you, and I was brought here by some apology for an angel who went screaming off the minute the fighting started. Then your father arrived, and that's when the *real* disaster happened.

LYRA. Let's see it.

He lays out the shattered pieces of the knife. She looks at them.

One, two, three, four . . .

WILL. Seven pieces. It was your dad. He made me think about my own father . . . and my thoughts got split, and the knife came up against something hard. And I forced it, and it flew into pieces.

LYRA. Iorek can fix it.

WILL. Can he? Can he really?

LYRA. Yeah, I bet he can! He can do more with metal than any bear alive, he told me. Come on, let's find him.

The CHEVALIER TIALYS and LADY SALMAKIA appear.

WILL. Hang on a minute. Look!

LYRA. Wow.

WILL. Are they normal size and far away?

LYRA. No, they're under our noses and they're tiny.

TIALYS. Good morning, Lyra. Good morning, Master Will.

WILL. Who are you?

LYRA. Whose side are you on?

TIALYS. I am the Chevalier Tialys, and this is my spouse, the Lady Salmakia. We are Gallivespians, and Lord Asriel's trusted spies.

SALMAKIA. We have been searching for you, Miss Lyra, at your father's command. (*To* TIALYS.) Will you continue, My Lord?

TIALYS. I yield to you, My Lady.

SALMAKIA. Too kind. Our orders are to take you to your father's fortress without delay. A gyropter will shortly arrive to collect us.

LYRA. What if I don't wanna go?

TIALYS. Our powers of persuasion are not inconsiderable. Have you forgotten the Gallivespians' notorious sting?

WILL. What about me? I've got an important message for Lord Asriel.

TIALYS. Your message is of no value, now that the knife is broken.

SALMAKIA. Which it certainly seems to be.

The GALLIVESPIANS *look at the pieces of the knife, which are still spread out.*

WILL. Yeah, I agree it looks pretty terrible. But there's an armoured bear, called Iorek Byrnison . . .

LYRA *interrupts hastily.*

LYRA. It's just broken bits of metal, isn't it? And the thing about the bear is, we just wanna say goodbye to him. Will you fetch him for us please?

TIALYS. Stay here, and we shall bring him to you.

SALMAKIA. But once we have done so, you must travel directly to Lord Asriel.

LYRA. Oh, I'll do that all right.

The GALLIVESPIANS *go.*

You're a hopeless, useless liar, Will. It's lucky I'm here. It's really important that those Gallipot-things don't know it's gonna be fixed.

WILL. Why not?

LYRA. 'Cause I don't wanna go to my father's, right? 'Cause he killed Roger. And there's something else that I gotta do, and that's about Roger too. I gotta rescue him.

WILL. Roger's dead!

LYRA. I know, but I seen him, Will. All that time I was asleep, I kept on having a dream. I was in this huge, grey, flat nothing of a place, and Roger was there. He was . . . beckoning to me, calling me, only I couldn't hear him. And he's only *there* because of me . . . and if I could find him, I could help him escape. Only I don't know where he is.

WILL. He's in the Land of the Dead.

LYRA. How do you know?

WILL. The angel told me. He said my father's gone there too.

LYRA. Then you gotta come with me, Will! We'll find them *both*! An' you can help your dad get out of that horrible place. You'll do it, won't you?

WILL. Yeah . . . I will . . . 'cause there's something I want to say to him, and I only thought of it when it was too late.

PANTALAIMON. How will you get there?

WILL. The knife'll cut us into it.

LYRA. 'Course it will!

PANTALAIMON. But . . .

WILL. Look, here's Iorek.

   IOREK *is there.*

IOREK. Lyra Silvertongue! You sent for me.

LYRA. Yeah, Will's got something very special to ask you.

WILL. Ssh, ssh, ssh, hang on. Can you see those little whatsits anywhere?

   They look round.

LYRA. No, they've gone.

WILL. You sure about that?

LYRA. Quite sure.

IOREK. What is your question?

   WILL *shows him the broken pieces of the knife.*

WILL. Can you mend this knife?

LYRA. I know you can!

> The CHEVALIER TIALYS *and* LADY SALMAKIA
> *appear from somewhere unexpected.*

SALMAKIA. This bear can mend it?

TIALYS. You've deceived us!

SALMAKIA. It was dishonourable to lie.

WILL. Well, you never asked permission to interrupt. This bear
happens to be a king, and you're just a couple of spies.

LYRA. And if you knew that we was lying, you'd have
probably killed us.

WILL. And we'd never have found the only creature in the
world who can actually fix it!

IOREK (*severely, to the* GALLIVESPIANS). Well?

TIALYS. Forgive us, Your Majesty. The habit of concealment
is hard to break. In our world, we live among larger humans
who are constantly attempting to exterminate us. Our
intentions towards yourself are wholly respectful.

SALMAKIA. We only intend to take these children to Lord
Asriel.

TIALYS. And the knife as well.

SALMAKIA. Once it is mended.

IOREK. Let me see it.

> WILL *shows him the pieces. He looks at them.*

I didn't trust this knife when I saw it before. I still don't like
it. It would be better if it had never been made.

LYRA. Oh, Iorek, if you only knew what we wanted to do with
it . . .

IOREK. Your intentions may be good. But the knife has its
own intentions. In doing what *you* want, you may also do
what the knife wants, without your knowing it. Look at this
edge. Can you see where it ends?

LYRA / WILL. No.

IOREK. Then how can you know where it will take you?

LYRA. I can ask the alethiometer.

IOREK. Ask it now. Then, if you still want me to mend it for you, I will do so.

TIALYS. May I respectfully say, Your Majesty, that the knife must be repaired whatever the child decides.

SALMAKIA. But we must not pre-empt the King.

TIALYS. How true, my dear. Let us withdraw to send Lord Asriel our dispatch.

They go.

LYRA. Can they hear us?

WILL. No.

She reads the alethiometer. IOREK watches.

IOREK. What does it say?

LYRA. It's . . . confused. It says the knife could be harmful, but it can also do good. But it's a tiny difference, like the littlest thought could tip it one way or the other.

WILL. What does it say about . . . the plan we made?

LYRA. It says it's dangerous.

WILL. What if we don't go?

LYRA. Just . . . blankness. Emptiness. Nothing.

WILL. How do we get there?

LYRA. It says, 'Follow the knife.'

IOREK. And is that what you want?

LYRA. It is.

IOREK. Then you must help me. Empty your mind of everything but the knife. Remember it as it was. I'll build a fire.

LORD ASRIEL's *fortress.* LORD ASRIEL, *with* STELMARIA *at his side, receives a message from the* CHEVALIER TIALYS *and* LADY SALMAKIA. LORD ROKE *is there.*

TIALYS. *The news is bad and good . . .*

SALMAKIA. *. . . . the knife is about to be repaired by an armoured bear, King Iorek Byrnison.*

LORD ASRIEL. Repaired?

TIALYS. *Lyra and the boy have promised to bring it to you once it is mended . . .*

The room erupts in triumph, as:

LORD ASRIEL. Yes! I've got it!

LORD ROKE. There's more, My Lord.

SALMAKIA. *But they are lying to us . . .*

LORD ASRIEL. What?

SALMAKIA. *. . . . they plan instead to travel to some unspecified location and to take it with them. Transmission over.*

LORD ASRIEL. The boy's betrayed me. Lord Roke, tell your spies to sting him to death, and bring me the knife themselves.

LORD ROKE. No, that won't help, My Lord. The knife is only effective in the hand of the Bearer.

LORD ASRIEL. Then they must bring him here by force.

LORD ROKE. No, that's not possible. Once the knife is in working order, he can't be forced to do anything. We've reached a deadlock.

LORD ASRIEL *flies into a rage.*

LORD ASRIEL. Damn those children! Damn the boy!

An OFFICER *appears at the door.*

OFFICER. My Lord, the prisoner insists on seeing you.

LORD ASRIEL. Not now! Send her away!

MRS COULTER *appears, her hands tied.*

MRS COULTER. Bound! Gagged! Dragged through your corridors like a criminal!

LORD ASRIEL. Oh, bring her in. Somebody free her. Everyone else, clear the room.

OFFICERS *bring her in.* MRS COULTER *protests to the* OFFICER *untying her.*

MRS COULTER. Gently! Gently!

LORD ASRIEL. Calm down!

MRS COULTER. Calm down? Don't you dare patronise me.

The OFFICER *untying her is the last person there.*

(*To him.*) Out! (*To* LORD ASRIEL.) Where's our daughter? What have you done with her?

LORD ASRIEL. I haven't done anything. She's back in the cave, where you saw her last.

MRS COULTER. You left her behind? While the battle was raging?

LORD ASRIEL. I would have rescued her if she'd had the wit to allow me to. But she ran away. Both she and the boy. They hid.

MRS COULTER. Didn't you look for her?

LORD ASRIEL. Of course I looked! Use your intelligence, Marisa. Why do you think I went to the cave in the first place?

MRS COULTER. Not for her. You've never minded whether she lived or died.

LORD ASRIEL. But now I do.

MRS COULTER. Well then, you'd better go back and get her.

LORD ASRIEL. I can't.

MRS COULTER. Why not?

LORD ASRIEL. Because like any other pair of selfish, self-indulgent children, they've placed their own concerns above the good of everyone else.

MRS COULTER. Just what does that mean exactly?

LORD ASRIEL. They plan to escape.

MRS COULTER. Escape from you, you mean.

LORD ASRIEL. And you.

MRS COULTER. So . . . where are they going?

LORD ASRIEL. I've no idea.

MRS COULTER. Has it crossed your mind that as long as Lyra is wandering free she'll be in terrible danger?

LORD ASRIEL. I know that.

MRS COULTER. *Now* you know it. Now you *admit* it. I tried to tell you that at Svalbard and you said I was talking nonsense.

LORD ASRIEL. That was nothing! There was a zeppelin overhead! A single zeppelin! It's different now. The Church is obsessed with her. They sent a party of suicide-killers to wipe her out. What's the prophecy?

MRS COULTER. The prophecy?

LORD ASRIEL. Yes, the witches' prophecy. What is it?

MRS COULTER. There's a name. A secret name. That name is the key to whether or not she's the Church's greatest enemy, and it's perfectly obvious that they've found it out and decided that she is.

LORD ASRIEL. Do you know this name?

MRS COULTER. I wish I did. I wish I thought that it mattered to you. You've never shown the remotest interest in her.

LORD ASRIEL. Why do you keep saying that? All I can think about, all I care about, night and day, is to find and protect that child who is so dear to us both.

MRS COULTER. I don't know why I believe you. You always lied in the past. I always knew it. But something's dulled in me. I've changed. Lyra has changed me. All those nights in the cave, feeding her, guarding her, listening in fear to every rustle of the wind . . . Well, that's all over.

She flexes her wrists.

So. We need that name, in order to fight the Church on equal terms. And we need to know where Lyra is, so you can bring her to safety. I think I'm getting somewhere. Who found the cave? Who knew that Will was there and the knife was there?

LORD ASRIEL. The Church's new alethiometer-reader.

MRS COULTER. Exactly. I've seen him. He's called Brother Jasper, and he's young and chillingly conscientious and there's nothing he can't find out. Can't your spies in Geneva sneak into his study and peek over his shoulder?

LORD ASRIEL. I haven't got any spies in Geneva. They're still at the cave. You saw them.

MRS COULTER. I *experienced* them.

She rubs her ankle.

Then you must send another spy. Someone who knows how their disgusting minds work . . . and whom they trust, up to a point. It will have to be me.

LORD ASRIEL. You? No, Marisa, it's impossible.

MRS COULTER. Oh, you're worried about my safety, are you?

LORD ASRIEL. I'm worried about your loyalty to me. You're the Church's faithful servant.

MRS COULTER. Not any more. I hate them. I hate them so intensely that it will be difficult for me to lie to them. But I'll manage it somehow. And I'll twist little Brother Jasper into telling me all he knows. I think I'll rather enjoy that. How do I get there?

LORD ASRIEL. My men will fly you there as soon as you're
    ready. They'll collect you the following morning at four
    a.m.

MRS COULTER. One moment.

She looks at the GOLDEN MONKEY, *who is making
stabbing gestures in the air.*

What?

He repeats the gesture.

(*To* LORD ASRIEL.) Just tell me one thing. What happened
to the knife?

LORD ASRIEL. The knife?

MRS COULTER. Yes, after it broke.

LORD ASRIEL. It will be mended.

MRS COULTER. *That's* what you're after, isn't it? *Isn't it?*
    You toad! You schemer! This is nothing to do with Lyra at
    all. It's the knife!

LORD ASRIEL. I need that knife!

MRS COULTER. What for? So you can kill the Authority?
    Ha ha ha. What good will that do? Have you thought about
    that? No, you don't care. It's all your pride, your glorification,
    your ambition . . . !

LORD ASRIEL. This is unworthy of you, Marisa.

MRS COULTER. Oh, come off it. How would you know
    what's worthy or not? You tried to exploit my motherly love
    for your own selfish purposes!

He laughs.

Don't laugh!

LORD ASRIEL. I can't help it!

He laughs.

Your motherly love! You hated Lyra! You abandoned her!

MRS COULTER. I did not! You stole her from me . . . !

LORD ASRIEL. I had to! You were raving mad! You'd have throttled her in her cradle!

MRS COULTER. Then you ignored her, you neglected her, year after year, she had no decent company, no education . . .

LORD ASRIEL. You only loved her in that cave because she was fast asleep.

MRS COULTER. What if I did? It's still love.

LORD ASRIEL. No it's not. It's fantasising. So that you won't have to *pretend* to love the tedious little creature that she really is.

MRS COULTER. You know nothing about her! She's unique!

LORD ASRIEL. Oh, she's unique all right. To win you round . . . you of all people . . . the steely-eyed fanatic, the persecutor of children, the inventor of hideous machines to slice them apart . . . to turn you into a fussy red hen, clucking and settling your feathers over her . . . that's quite an achievement.

MRS COULTER. It is.

LORD ASRIEL. And you'll go to Geneva?

MRS COULTER. I will. For her.

She turns to go.

Who won that? You or me?

LORD ASRIEL. We both got what we wanted.

MRS COULTER. So we did. But I'll be back. And then let battle commence.

She goes out. LORD ROKE, *who has been hiding somewhere, appears.*

LORD ROKE. My Lord?

LORD ASRIEL. Hide in the aircraft. Don't let her see you. Report to me when you get there.

In the cave. IOREK *is mending the knife.* LYRA, WILL *and* PANTALAIMON *are helping.*

IOREK (*to* WILL). Last piece! Hold it still in your mind!

    WILL *concentrates on his mental image of the knife.*

WILL. I've got it! I can see it!

IOREK. Feel the atoms! Feel them joining, strengthening, straightening!

WILL. I feel them!

    IOREK *hammers the last fragments into place.*

IOREK. Now it must cool. Lyra, call me when the blade turns back to silver.

    He places it in the cinders.

    (*To* WILL.) Come.

    He and WILL *walk out of the cave.*

    What will you do with the knife?

WILL. I don't know.

    IOREK *knocks him over.*

IOREK. Answer me truthfully.

    WILL *struggles to his feet.*

WILL. We want to go down to the Land of the Dead . . . for my father, and Roger as well. But I'm pulled in so many different ways. My mum's ill, and I want to go home and look after her. My father told me to take the knife to Lord Asriel. And I'm frightened . . . and maybe my fear is pushing me in the wrong direction. Maybe sometimes the frightening thing is the wrong thing, but we don't want to look like a coward, and so we do it *because* it's frightening.

IOREK. I too am full of doubt. And that is a human thing. If I am becoming human, something's wrong, something's bad. It may be that I have brought the final destruction on my kingdom. But there is one thing I know for certain. If you want to succeed in the task you have set yourself, you must no longer think about your father and mother. If your mind is divided, the knife will break once more, and I will not be there to mend it.

LYRA *approaches.*

LYRA. Iorek, the knife is ready.

IOREK. Will has told me where you are going.

LYRA. I've gotta rescue Roger.

IOREK. Your business is not with death. It is with living creatures.

LYRA. Our business is to do what we promised, en't it? I wish I'd never had that dream, and I wish we'd never found out that the knife could take us there. But it can.

IOREK. Can is not the same as must.

LYRA. But if you must, and you can, then you got no excuse.

IOREK. I was right to call you Lyra Silvertongue. You've made me change my mind. (*To* WILL.) Take the knife, and plunge it into the stream.

WILL *goes to do so.*

(*To* LYRA.) When I first met him, he was too clever for me, too daring. There is no one else I would be happy to leave you with. If you escape from the Land of the Dead, you will meet me in the battle at the end of the world. If you cannot escape, you'll never see me again. I have no ghost. When I die, my body will lie on the earth, and then be part of it. Go well.

LYRA. Go well, King Iorek Byrnison.

She embraces him and he goes. WILL *comes back with the knife.*

WILL. It's done. It'll work.

She looks at it.

LYRA. It isn't beautiful any more.

WILL. It looks what it is. It's wounded.

WILL prepares to cut a window.

LYRA. Right, let's go there.

PANTALAIMON. What if you can't get out?

LYRA. If it can cut us in, it'll cut us out again.

PANTALAIMON. What if you gotta die to be there?

WILL. We aren't gonna die. Not with our bodies. 'Cause bodies don't go anywhere. They just stay in the earth and rot.

LYRA. And it can't be our daemons either. They just fade and dissolve.

PANTALAIMON. I don't wanna fade and dissolve!

LYRA. You won't have to, Pan, 'cause there must be a different part. A part that's not our bodies, an' not our daemons. A part that can think about both those things. A third part.

WILL. Our ghost.

LYRA. That's right. Our ghost. We're going as ghosts.

PANTALAIMON. Ghosts are sad! Ghosts are frightening! Don't go!

LYRA. Oh Pan . . . we won't know anything till we try it. You know I love you. I'll look after you for ever an' ever. But we can't be too frightened to do what we've got to.

WILL. Let's go.

He tries a snag in the air: it feels wrong.

Not that.

The CHEVALIER TIALYS and LADY SALMAKIA appear.

TIALYS. Where do you think you are going, young man?

LYRA. Oh, no!

WILL. We're gonna follow the knife to the Land of the Dead.

TIALYS. You may not do that!

SALMAKIA. You must wait for the gyropter.

WILL. It doesn't matter what you think. We're going. You can come if you like, or stay where you are. It's up to you.

He stretches out his hand, holding the knife. Tries a couple of snags.

Not that. Not that.

As he looks for a place to cut, the CHEVALIER TIALYS *and* LADY SALMAKIA *try to stop him.*

TIALYS (*simultaneously with* SALMAKIA). This is forbidden. The entire destiny of the universe is at stake. You must follow Lord Asriel's orders. We are speaking on his behalf. You may not defy us. You must carry out your mission. You may not deviate, not in the slightest. It is rank insubordination. It is tantamount to treason. You will regret it! You'll be very, very sorry unless you stop at once! Put down that knife! Replace it where it belongs! Stop this immediately! Stop it at once! This instant!

SALMAKIA. You may not do this. It is a direct contravention of the rules for prisoners. Put down that knife immediately. You are in our custody. You must do precisely as we command you. We have explained this very clearly. How dare you be so disobedient? How dare you? Don't you know who we are? It's an outrage. It's atrocious behaviour. You have brought disgrace on the entire Gallivespian nation. We shall punish you frightfully. I order you to do as we say! Do as we say!

WILL *tries another.*

WILL. This could be it.

The feeling is unpleasant.

You sure about this?

LYRA. Go on.

He cuts a window. They stare in amazement at what they see through it.

A lodestone resonator signal from the CHEVALIER TIALYS.

TIALYS. *The Chevalier Tialys regrets to inform you . . . Lyra and the boy have escaped with the knife to the Land of the Dead after overpowering your agents and issuing violent threats . . .*

The signal cross-fades with another signal.

LORD ROKE. *Lord Roke reporting from Geneva . . . Mrs Coulter arrived purporting to bring vital information damaging to Your Lordship. This claim was greeted with mistrust. She has been placed in a cell, where the President will shortly arrive to interrogate her.*

The Consistorial Court of Discipline. MRS COULTER *is in a cell. She's about to undress when she sees* LORD ROKE.

MRS COULTER. Lord Roke! Just when would you have done me the courtesy of telling me you were here? Before I undressed or after?

LORD ROKE. Before, of course. Do you really suppose I have some unseemly interest in giantesses? I've toured the grounds. They're preparing for war. The priests are taking it in relays to warn the Authority.

MRS COULTER. How?

LORD ROKE. Incense, bells, whatever they can lay their hands on.

MRS COULTER. Has Brother Jasper found out where Lyra is?

LORD ROKE. I think not yet. He's looking worried.

A knock at the door.

See for yourself.

MRS COULTER. Quick, hide.

LORD ROKE *conceals himself.*

Come in.

The PRESIDENT *and* BROTHER JASPER *enter.*

PRESIDENT. Welcome, Mrs Coulter. Forgive this simple hospitality. Once you have proved that you are truly the Church's friend, and not a traitor, you'll have better lodgings.

MRS COULTER (*to* BROTHER JASPER). I believe we've met.

PRESIDENT. Brother Jasper is here to ensure that I do not waste our time by asking you questions which can be more swiftly answered by the alethiometer.

MRS COULTER. Well, he's a great improvement on Fra Pavel, in all sorts of ways. I'm so sorry. Ask me whatever you like.

PRESIDENT. I'm bound to wonder how you escaped from Lord Asriel's fortress with such ease, and how you came to Geneva?

MRS COULTER. As I told your guards, I stole a gyropter. I landed it in the countryside not far from here, and the rest of the way I walked.

PRESIDENT. What can you tell me about the mysterious disappearance of Lord Boreal?

MRS COULTER. He and I were in Cittàgazze, and the Spectres killed him. It's what happens there.

PRESIDENT. To what do you attribute your own survival?

MRS COULTER. The power of prayer.

PRESIDENT. You've offered to brief us on Lord Asriel's plans. In fact, we know them all. But there is one important question still outstanding.

MRS COULTER. Which is?

PRESIDENT. Where's your daughter?

MRS COULTER. I've no idea. Why don't you ask the alethiometer?

The PRESIDENT *glances at* BROTHER JASPER.

BROTHER JASPER. I have done so. But the answer is too obscure for me to read.

MRS COULTER (*to* BROTHER JASPER). Well, once you've worked out what it's saying, I beg you to tell me. I'm Lyra's mother. I have the right to know.

PRESIDENT. We would be more impressed by your maternal feelings if you hadn't misused them so atrociously!

MRS COULTER. What?

The PRESIDENT *gets increasingly angry.*

PRESIDENT. You persuaded me to let you search for Lyra. I made *one* condition. You were to tell us when you had found her. You disobeyed. You hid her in a cave. You forced me to send the flower of the Church's youth in her pursuit, and many of them died. What was your motive? Were you protecting her? If so, from what?

MRS COULTER *loses control.*

MRS COULTER. From a body of men with a feverish obsession with sex, that's what.

PRESIDENT. I beg your pardon?

MRS COULTER. You heard me. Men whose furtive imaginations would crawl over my daughter like cockroaches. Men reeking of ancient sweat!

PRESIDENT. You have one last chance to save yourself. Lord Asriel plans to kill the Authority. Does that appal you? Does it fill you with horror and fear?

MRS COULTER. I think, what does it matter? The Authority's useless. Nobody sees him. Nobody hears him. Nobody cares what he thinks. The wicked get rich, and the poor and humble die in their millions without so much as a squeak of protest. *If* he's alive, he's clearly too old and decrepit

to think or to act or even die. Wouldn't it be the kindest
gesture to seek him out and give him the gift of death?

PRESIDENT. 'Out of their own mouths they shall condemn
themselves.' Good night.

He and BROTHER JASPER *leave.*

MRS COULTER. Oh, that was *stupid*!

We follow the PRESIDENT *and* BROTHER JASPER.

PRESIDENT. It is imperative that we find the child. Has the
alethiometer told you nothing?

BROTHER JASPER. That is *exactly* what it has told me,
Father President. Nothing. Emptiness. An all-extending,
malevolent grey. I simply can't work out what world it is
trying to describe.

PRESIDENT. You will continue your enquiries. As for the
woman, she will die tomorrow. I fear confession will be of
little advantage to her, but we must do what we can. Return
to her cell after the Council of War, and hear her final
words.

BROTHER JASPER. But Father President, the lady will be in
bed. Father President?

Outskirts of the Land of the Dead. The sound of sea birds.
GHOSTS *are arriving.* LYRA, WILL *and* PANTALAIMON
arrive. An official, MR PERKINS, *is there at a desk. He has a
clipboard.*

PERKINS. Excuse me! You people are still alive.

He prepares papers for them.

You wouldn't believe the number of living people they're
sending us these days. Take these papers through to the
holding area . . . make yourselves known . . . and wait.

LYRA. How long for?

PERKINS. Until you die, of course.

WILL. And then what happens?

PERKINS. Then you'll be travelling on by boat.

WILL. Where to?

PERKINS. I'm not permitted to tell you that. Proceed down there, first gate on the left.

(*To an* ANONYMOUS QUEUE *waiting for attention.*) Move on. Who's next? (*Facetious.*) Look alive!

WILL *and* LYRA *walk away.*

WILL. Do you reckon this is it?

LYRA. It en't what I saw in my dream. It's more like a transit place.

WILL. Papers! Look at 'em. They're just pages torn out of an exercise book.

LYRA. At least he didn't look dangerous.

PANTALAIMON. *All* of it's dangerous. Let's go back. I wanna go back.

LYRA. Ssh . . . ! (*She calls.*) Hello?

A man, JEPTHA JONES, *is there.*

Is this all right? We was told to come in. I'm Lyra and this is Will. And this is my daemon, Pantalaimon.

JEPTHA *looks at them, puzzled.*

JEPTHA. You haven't brought your deaths with you.

LYRA. Our *deaths*?

WILL. No, we haven't. (*Quietly, to* LYRA.) What's he talkin' about?

LYRA. Dunno.

They follow JEPTHA *to where his family is sitting on camping chairs: his wife* HANNAH, OLD MOTHER JONES, *her* DEATH *and a* YOUNG BOY.

We're sorry we've come without our deaths, if that's the normal way of things. But we hope you can help us. We're looking for the Land of the Dead, and we don't know how to get there. So if you can tell us about it, we'll be really grateful.

JEPTHA. Come and sit down.

LYRA / WILL. Thank you very much.

JEPTHA. I'm Jeptha Jones. Hannah, I think they're hungry.

They come to the fire. HANNAH *pours soup into mugs for them.*

LYRA. Excuse me for asking, but are you dead?

JEPTHA (*a bit hurt*). Certainly not. Do you think we look it?

HANNAH. We're still alive, like you. We're waiting here until our deaths tell us it's time to go.

LYRA. Where are they?

HANNAH. They're there.

She indicates a little group of ANONYMOUS FIGURES *sitting apart from them.*

They don't bother us much. They keep themselves to themselves.

JEPTHA. Except for our gran's.

OLD MOTHER JONES'S DEATH, *who is as old as the gran, looks up.*

Hello, old pal. Giving her a nice cuppa soup, are you?

MOTHER JONES'S DEATH *nods.*

MOTHER JONES'S DEATH. I am, I am.

JEPTHA (*to* LYRA). Before we arrived, we never could see our deaths. We always had them, though, like everyone else.

LYRA. What, all the time?

HANNAH. Oh yes. Your death comes into the world with you the minute you're born, and it stays with you every minute

of your days, until it's time to go. It could come at any
moment. When you're sick with a fever, or you choke on
a piece of dry bread, or you stand at the top of a high
building. In the middle of all your pain and hardship, your
death comes to you kindly and says . . . 'Easy now, easy,
child, you come along o' me.' And then it shows you into
a boat, and out you sail.

LYRA. Where to?

HANNAH. Nobody knows.

LYRA. If I want to get on to that boat . . . how can I find it?

HANNAH. You must call up your death.

LYRA (*frightened*). Will I see it? See it in front of me?

HANNAH. It's the only way. *He'll* tell you.

They look at MOTHER JONES'S DEATH. *He chuckles.*

MOTHER JONES'S DEATH. I've heard of people like you,
my gal. You don't want to know about your deaths. That's
why we stay out of sight. It's our good manners. But we're
always there. You turn your head, and we dodge behind you.
We can hide in a teacup, or a dewdrop, or in a breath of
wind. But we get a bit bolder once your time comes near.

He pinches MOTHER JONES*'s cheek.*

I never stray far from you these days, do I, sweetie?

LYRA. What do I do, to call up my death?

MOTHER JONES'S DEATH. Just wish.

PANTALAIMON. Don't. Don't!

LYRA. I'm wishing.

They all look round.

JEPTHA. Nothing.

HANNAH. Just as well, eh? A child like her. Drink your soup.

They drink soup.

JEPTHA. It's strange you got here. How did it happen?

LYRA. Well, my mum and dad was a king and a queen . . . and they were thrown in prison . . .

HANNAH. So you're a princess?

LYRA. . . . and they shimmied down a rope. With me in their arms, 'cause I was just a baby. We was attacked by outlaws, and they would've roasted and eaten me, except I was rescued by Will. He'd fallen off the side of a ship, and he was washed up on a desolate shore and suckled by wolves . . . An' then . . .

The actor playing PANTALAIMON *appears as* LYRA'S DEATH.

HANNAH. That's him.

LYRA. Are you my death?

LYRA'S DEATH. Yes, my dear.

LYRA. But you're not gonna take me?

LYRA'S DEATH. Don't you want me to? I thought you wished.

LYRA. I did . . . but I don't want to die, not yet.

LYRA'S DEATH. I can wait. You'll go to the Land of the Dead in your own good time. And when you do, instead of your daemon, you'll have another friend, a special, devoted friend, who you don't know at all. But I'll have been with you every moment of your life. I know you better than you do yourself.

LYRA. You don't understand. I want to go there now . . . but I wanna come back.

LYRA'S DEATH. Nobody's ever come back, not for many a year. Why should you be any different?

LYRA. I had someone taken away from me.

WILL. Me too.

LYRA'S DEATH. Everyone wants to see those people who've gone before. And if that is truly what you want, then I can show you the way. But as for returning . . . there I can't help you. You must manage on your own. Do you still want to go?

LYRA. Will?

WILL. Let's do it.

HANNAH. Good luck, dear.

JEPTHA. Safe journey.

HANNAH. Hope you find what you're looking for.

LYRA'S DEATH. Follow me.

As they leave, GHOSTS *and* DEATHS *bid them goodbye.*

GHOSTS / DEATHS. Goodbye. / Take care. / I hope you know what you're doing.

LYRA *and* WILL *walk on and reach the shores of a lake.*

LYRA'S DEATH. This is as far as I can take you. Wait here.

He disappears.

LYRA. Listen.

A rowing boat is heard.

WILL. It's the boat.

LYRA. Will? You ready?

PANTALAIMON *howls.*

Ssh, Pan.

The boat appears and comes to rest, rowed by a very old BOATMAN.

WILL. I'll go first.

PANTALAIMON. No!

BOATMAN. Not him.

LYRA. Not who?

The BOATMAN *indicates* PANTALAIMON.

I can't leave Pantalaimon behind. I'll die!

BOATMAN. Isn't that what you want?

PANTALAIMON *howls and whimpers.*

WILL. No, that's not fair. Her daemon is part of her. I don't
have to leave part of myself behind.

BOATMAN. You do, young man. The only difference is that
she can see it and talk to it. You will lose something just as
precious, and you'll miss it as much as she does.

LYRA. How will I find him again?

BOATMAN. You never will.

LYRA. What if he waits for us here, and we come back this
way?

BOATMAN. You won't come back this way, nor any other.

LYRA. Will?

WILL (*to the* BOATMAN). You're wrong. We will come back.
We'll be the first since nearly ever. So what's the point of
splitting up people and their daemons for the sake of a
stupid rule? Let him come with us, just this once.

BOATMAN. 'Just this once!' If only you knew how often I've
heard those words. How many people do you think I've
taken across this lake? Millions. Millions, millions. There's
not one of 'em does it gladly. They struggle, they cry, they
try to bribe me, they threaten and fight. They say they're not
really dead, that it's all a mistake. They tell me about the
gold and silver they've scraped together, and their powerful
friends, the King of this and the Duke of that. And they all
of them say that, just this once, the rules have got to be
changed. They soon find out there's only one rule that
matters. That they're in my boat, and I'm rowing that boat
to the Land of the Dead, and I'll be rowing those kings and
dukes as well before they know it. They're just the same as
everyone else that breathes. And so are you.

WILL. Lyra!

LYRA embraces PANTALAIMON.

LYRA. Pan, I love you. If I have to spend the rest of my life finding you again, I will. But I can't go back. I can't. I'm gonna push you away now. I'm sorry.

She pushes PANTALAIMON *away and steps on to the boat. WILL steps in after.* PANTALAIMON *crouches, forlorn and desolate. The* BOATMAN *pushes off and the boat moves away from the shore.* LYRA *and* PANTALAIMON *feel the pain of separation.* LYRA *cries in agony.*

Oh Pan!

A message is seen / heard from LORD ROKE.

LORD ROKE. *Lord Roke reporting from Geneva. Information regarding Lyra, Will or the knife amounts to nil. Preparations for war continue apace. Mrs Coulter unfortunately blew her cover and is now under sentence of death. She awaits the arrival of the rescue party with impatience.*

Geneva. MRS COULTER*'s cell.* MRS COULTER *is pacing up and down anxiously.* LORD ROKE *appears in the window.*

LORD ROKE. Mrs Coulter! Mrs Coulter! Brother Jasper is on his way to see you.

MRS COULTER. What does he want?

LORD ROKE. Who knows? But it's your last chance to find out anything useful, so do please give it your best shot.

There is a knock on the door.

MRS COULTER. Ssh!

LORD ROKE *gets out of sight.* MRS COULTER *stretches out on the bed. She yawns and replies as though awoken from a deep sleep.*

Come in.

BROTHER JASPER comes in with the alethiometer.

BROTHER JASPER. Mrs Coulter! Forgive my awakening you so late at night. I bring you wonderful news. This medallion . . .

He removes it from around his neck.

. . . confers forgiveness for all crimes past and present. No one has greater need of it than you. I will give it to you, and you will die as pure as a newborn child, if you can help me find your daughter.

MRS COULTER. Well, naturally I accept. But how can I help?

BROTHER JASPER. Just tell me: who is Roger?

MRS COULTER. *Roger?* He was a friend of Lyra's when she lived in Oxford.

BROTHER JASPER. And where is he now?

MRS COULTER. I'm not sure I know how to answer that. Why do you ask?

BROTHER JASPER. Because I don't understand what the alethiometer is trying to tell me. Lyra has gone to look for this Roger in a world of endless grey and misery. Tell me where he is, and then I shall know where Lyra is . . . and you will bask forever in the bliss of the holy vision.

MRS COULTER. Roger isn't anywhere. He's dead.

BROTHER JASPER (*appalled*). Dead? *Dead?* No, that's impossible. Death is a place of infinite light and joy. If that's not true, then *nothing* is true!

He falls to his knees in great distress.

Save me! Don't let me believe her!

The GOLDEN MONKEY moves seductively towards BROTHER JASPER'S DAEMON, who responds shyly.

MRS COULTER. Oh Jasper, don't be upset. The moment I saw you, I knew you were different from the others. You have the courage to doubt a little. You have a human heart. But you've forgotten something.

He moves to place the medallion round her neck, but hesitates before touching her. She takes it and puts it on. He stays where he is, uncomfortably close to her, but unable to move away.

Just tell me this: where Lyra's gone, is the boy with the knife there too?

BROTHER JASPER. Yes.

MRS COULTER. Can you follow them there?

BROTHER JASPER. No.

MRS COULTER. And why do you want to kill her? What is her name?

Her GOLDEN MONKEY *embraces his* DAEMON *lovingly.*

BROTHER JASPER. It's Eve. The woman who . . . tempted the man. When they embraced the . . . ways of the flesh . . . and fell.

MRS COULTER. And then?

BROTHER JASPER. We lost our innocence. And then Dust entered the world, and we've been fighting it ever since.

MRS COULTER. So Lyra and Will are Eve and Adam? And that's what it's all about? You're trying to stop them?

BROTHER JASPER. Yes! If Lyra falls, it will happen again. The Triumph of Dust.

Gunshots are heard from outside. LORD ROKE *appears.*

LORD ROKE. The rescue party's arrived!

The GOLDEN MONKEY *fixes* BROTHER JASPER'S DAEMON *in a grip, paralysing her.* MRS COULTER *flings* BROTHER JASPER *away from her. He falls to the ground and writhes in pain.*

MRS COULTER (*to* BROTHER JASPER). They lied, little man! Death is emptiness. Blankness. Nothing.

SOLDIERS *of* LORD ASRIEL *enter and hustle her to the door. Armed* CLERICS *enter and fire.* LORD ROKE *is wounded.*

LORD ROKE. Run, My Lady! Don't wait for me! When you see Lord Asriel, tell him I stayed at my post!

The Land of the Dead. The boat pulls up at a jetty and WILL *and* LYRA *climb out; the* GALLIVESPIANS *hover nearby. Harsh bird-like cries are heard. The* BOATMAN *rows away.*

LYRA. Do you feel it, Will? A big empty space where your daemon was?

WILL. It's worse than empty. It's like a fist punched through my ribs and pulled something out.

There's a door.

LYRA. We can't stay here.

WILL. Better go through.

A harpy, NO-NAME, *appears.*

NO-NAME. You are alive! And so-o-o-o sad!

She laughs.

LYRA. What's that?

WILL. It's a harpy. I've seen 'em in books.

NO-NAME. Your mother went mad! And you were so-o-o-o ashamed of her!

WILL. Yeah, well you better be able to fight as well as scream, 'cause we're going through that door!

NO-NAME. Will's mummy is having nightmares! She's all alone! Ha ha ha ha!

LYRA. Let us through!

NO-NAME. You weren't Roger's friend! You thought he was thick! You just wanted to see your daddy, and Roger died!

She shrieks with laughter.

LYRA. Who are you? What's your name?

NO-NAME. No name!

LYRA. What do you want with us, No-Name?

NO-NAME. What can you do for me?

LYRA. We could tell you where we've been. You might be
    interested.

NO-NAME. You mean, you'll tell me a story?

LYRA. Yeah.

NO-NAME. Tell me a story I like, and I might let you through.

LYRA. All right. My mother and father were the Duke and
    Duchess of Abingdon, and they was as rich as anything. The
    King used to come and hunt tigers in our enormous forest.
    And . . .

    NO-NAME *launches herself at* LYRA.

NO-NAME. Liar! Lyra the liar, Lyra the liar, Lyra the liar!

    WILL *extends the knife. The* HARPY *swoops away*

LYRA. What's happening, Will? Why can't I lie any more?

WILL. Through here.

WILL *slices through the door. They run through it into a vast
grey plain.* HARPIES *cry overhead. The plain is peopled with*
GHOSTS: *sitting, crouching, all grey and listless.*

WILL. Look!

LYRA. It's the place in my dream.

WILL. Are these the ghosts?

LYRA. Yeah. This is everyone in all the worlds who ever died.

WILL. So many kids. It's so sad.

LYRA. Will . . . I just thought of something. When Mr Scoresby was flying me from Bolvangar, Serafina was talking about me, 'cause she thought I was asleep. There's a prophecy about me. I'm gonna do something special. Something to do with death. A nyal . . . A nyler . . .

WILL. Annihilation. Making something into nothing.

LYRA. That's what I'll do. I'm gonna finish off death for good. Not just Roger, not just your father. All of them, every one. We're gonna cut a window into the world outside, and let the ghosts go free. So you better make sure that the knife can get us out.

WILL. I'll find some place where they aren't all staring at us.

He turns to go.

LYRA. Will.

WILL. What?

LYRA. I'm glad we're here together.

WILL. Yeah, me too.

He goes. CHILDREN *approach* LYRA.

1ST GHOST-CHILD. You! You're a new kid, aren't you?

2ND GHOST-CHILD. Do you miss your daemon?

LYRA. Yeah. But I'm getting him back.

1ST GHOST-CHILD. Everyone thinks that when they've just arrived.

3RD GHOST-CHILD. Don't get any better either.

2ND GHOST-CHILD. We're always thinking about daemons, en't we?

1ST GHOST-CHILD. Yeah, we sit and remember 'em all the time.

2ND GHOST-CHILD. My daemon . . .

3RD GHOST-CHILD. Yeah?

2ND GHOST-CHILD. . . . he used to think he'd settle as a
bird, but I hoped he wouldn't, 'cause I liked stroking his fur.

1ST GHOST-CHILD. My daemon and me used to play hide-
and-seek.

Other GHOST CHILDREN *join in.*

GHOST-CHILDREN.
Mine used to curl up in my hand and go to sleep.

I hurt my eye and I couldn't see, and he guided me all the
way home.

Mine never wanted to settle, but I wanted to grow up, and
we used to argue.

My daemon said, 'I'm over and done with,' then he went
forever. Just dissolved in the air. Now I ain't got him no
more. I don't know what's going to happen ever again.

There ain't *nothing* going to happen.

You don't know that!

That boy and this girl came, didn't they?

That's the first thing that's happened in years and years!

Nobody knew that *that* was going to happen.

Well, maybe it's all going to change now.

Yes! P'raps it'll change.

ROGER *appears.*

ROGER. Lyra!

LYRA. Rodge!

He runs to her.

ROGER. You've come to get me. I knew you would. I been
calling for you ever since I died. The others was making fun
of me every time, but I went on saying your name . . .

LYRA. I heard you.

ROGER. How? How did you hear me?

LYRA. I dreamed about you. I tried to hug you, but my arms went right through the air . . .

She reaches for him. He steps back and the HARPIES *chuckle maliciously.*

ROGER. You can't even touch a person here, it's a terrible place. There's nothing changes, it's just grey and hopeless, and them bird-things . . . they come up behind you, and they whisper all the bad things you ever did. All the greedy and 'orrible thoughts you ever had, they know them all. You can't get away from 'em.

LYRA. Don't worry, Rodge. I'm getting you out of here. Will's got a knife. It cuts through anything. And . . .

ROGER. Who's Will?

LYRA. My friend.

ROGER. Is he your best friend? Is he better than me?

LYRA. Not better, Rodge. No one could be better than what you were. He's just . . . the best friend I can touch . . . or hug . . .

ROGER. Tell me about it.

LYRA. Won't it make you sad?

ROGER. It might do . . . but at least it'll feel alive.

LYRA. Well . . . Will's the best friend I can get into fights with. Or share an apple with, or race up a hill, or sit in the sun.

The GHOST-CHILDREN *cluster nearer.*

GHOST-CHILDREN.
Tell us about it!

Tell us about the world!

We've half-forgotten it, miss!

Tell us!

LYRA *looks round: the* GHOST-CHILDREN *are clustered around her, listening.*

LYRA. I said 'fight', 'cause Roger and me used to fight the other kids in the Oxford clay-beds.

ROGER *smiles.*

ROGER. Yeah, we did.

LYRA. There's a row of willow trees along the side of the river, with the leaves all silvery underneath. Even in summer, when it's boiling hot, it's shady down there, and the clay is all sloshy and wet, but dry on top, so you can take a big slab in your hand like this.

ROGER *shows them.*

ROGER. Like that!

LYRA. And there's a million different smells there. Like smoke from where the bricks are burning . . .

ROGER. . . . and the river all warm and mouldy.

LYRA. . . . and the baked potatoes that the burners ate . . .

ROGER. Yeah, horrible food they eat . . .

LYRA. . . . and there'd be Roger, me, Simon Parslow . . .

ROGER. That's my cousin . . .

LYRA. . . . Hugh Lovett, the butler's son . . .

ROGER. . . . and Dick Purser, who could spit the furthest.

The CHILDREN *laugh.*

LYRA. Then when the clay was all over us head to foot . . .

She continues. Meanwhile:

Another part of the Land of the Dead. WILL *extends the knife into the air, looks for a snag. He finds one and tries to cut. There's a hideous, grating noise.* WILL *is about to try again.* JOPARI *appears.*

JOPARI. Do that once more, and the knife will break.

WILL. Father!

JOPARI. Will.

WILL. Aren't you angry with me? I didn't do what you said.

JOPARI. There's no time to talk. You've got to get out. There may be a cleft in the rocks above us, but it'll be a long and difficult climb to find it. Where's Lyra?

WILL. How did you know about Lyra?

JOPARI. I was a shaman, Will. And a father too. We know these things.

WILL. Follow me.

They see LYRA, *who is finishing her story. Grown-up* GHOSTS *are listening as well as* CHILDREN. NO-NAME *and two other* HARPIES *listen on the perimeter.*

LYRA. . . . and washed . . . and scrubbed . . . and put into bed. And we'd none of us had a more beautiful day in all our lives.

ROGER. That's how it was.

The CHILDREN *applaud quietly.*

LYRA. Here, No-Name, you enjoyed that. When I told you a story before, you flew at me.

NO-NAME. Because it was lies! Lies and fantasies!

LYRA. But now you was listening quietly. Why was that?

NO-NAME. Because you spoke the truth.

2ND HARPY. Because it was nourishing.

3RD HARPY. Because it was feeding us. Because we didn't know that there was anything in the world but lies and wickedness.

2ND HARPY. Because it brought us news of the wind and the sun and the rain.

NO-NAME. But now we've read your thoughts. You plan to escape. And there'll be no more stories! Traitor!

The HARPIES *scream and fly at* LYRA, *terrifying the* GHOSTS. WILL *leaps in towards* LYRA, *brandishing the knife, and the* HARPIES *draw back, squawking menacingly.*

LYRA. Will! Will! Will! Cut the window!

WILL. I can't! The knife won't work! We're stuck!

LYRA. No!

The HARPIES *scream in triumph.*

NO-NAME. We'll revenge ourselves! We made this place a wasteland. Now we'll make it hell!

3RD HARPY. We'll hurt you!

2ND HARPY. We'll defile you!

3RD HARPY. We'll send you mad with fear!

NO-NAME. We'll torture you every day until you tell us stories!

The HARPIES *advance on* LYRA *and* WILL.

WILL. Stop! We'll make a bargain. Show Lyra and me and all these ghosts the way to climb out of this place into the open air. And then for ever after . . . you'll have the right to lead every ghost who arrives, all the way through the Land of the Dead, from the landing post to the world outside.

NO-NAME. That's no bargain! What do we get in return?

LYRA. I'll tell you. Every one of those ghosts will have a story. They'll have *true* stories to tell you about the things they saw and heard and loved in the life that they left behind. You can ask them about their lives. And they gotta tell you.

NO-NAME. What if they won't? What if they lie? Can we torture them for ever?

LYRA glances at WILL, *who nods discreetly.*

LYRA. That's fair. Now show us the way!

A GHOST *steps forward.*

1ST GHOST. Not so fast. What will happen to us outside?

Other GHOSTS *join in anxiously.*

2ND GHOST. We'll never survive!

3RD GHOST. We won't exist!

1ST GHOST. We'll be better off down here.

3RD GHOST. Tell us what to expect!

2ND GHOST. We won't go one step until you tell us!

JOPARI steps forward.

JOPARI. Listen to me, all of you. We will dissolve, just like
    your daemons did when you died. But they're not *nothing*,
    They've gone into the wind and the trees and the earth and
    all the living things. That's what will happen to us, I swear
    to you. I promise you on my honour. We'll drift apart, but
    we'll be out in the open, part of everything that's alive.
    Well, what do you say?

NO-NAME spreads her wings.

NO-NAME. Follow me!

She moves away. The GHOSTS *follow.* JOPARI *gestures to
put his arm round* LYRA *as they go.*

Geneva. MRS COULTER*'s cell.* BROTHER JASPER *is there,
in despair. The* PRESIDENT *paces about in agitation.*

PRESIDENT. No! No! Since Lyra is who we know she is, she
    might *escape* the Land of the Dead. It's even possible that
    she'll . . .

BROTHER JASPER. What, Father President?

PRESIDENT. It's too horrible to contemplate. If she could
    free the dead . . . if she could bring them into the world
    outside . . .

Voices are heard approaching.

1ST CLERIC. He's here! He's with Brother Jasper!

2ND CLERIC. Tell him the news!

3RD CLERIC. Father President!

PRESIDENT. Who's calling?

> CLERICS *come in, armed for battle.* LORD ROKE, *who is wounded, creeps out of his hiding-place to listen.*

1ST CLERIC. A miracle has happened! The Clouded Mountain has appeared!

All but the PRESIDENT *fall to their knees.*

PRESIDENT. Who saw it?

3RD CLERIC. I did, Your Holiness. Like an enormous bank of clouds . . . sailing across the sky towards Lord Asriel's fortress . . . with cannons pointing out from the turrets, and lightning flashing and angels . . . !

PRESIDENT. Angels!

3RD CLERIC. . . . loyal angels, whirling and swooping around like a million birds.

PRESIDENT. The Authority is advancing! Is not this the sternest rebuke to those who claimed he was feeble or sick or dead? He is alive! He commands his troops. He wields the sword of retribution! Praise be!

CLERICS. Praise be!

PRESIDENT. Prepare to support him on the ground. The power of righteousness be with you all. Go!

They start to go. BROTHER JASPER *stays.*

BROTHER JASPER. Father President, let me speak. I have sinned. I had evil thoughts.

PRESIDENT. You are not the first young man to have been corrupted by Mrs Coulter. Make up for it on the battlefield.

BROTHER JASPER. No!

PRESIDENT. Do you refuse me?

BROTHER JASPER. There's something else that I can do. A task far greater than anything that our army can accomplish. They won't find Lyra. She's escaped us over and over. The knife can cut her into any one of a million worlds. But I've got this.

He produces the alethiometer.

It will guide me to her, swift as the arrow of God. Wherever she's gone, wherever the boy can lead her. I'll strike her down, like the angel that blasted the Assyrians. Give me your blessing. Let me go.

An armed CLERIC appears at the door.

CLERIC. Father President, the Council is assembled.

PRESIDENT. Give me that.

He takes the CLERIC's rifle, and gives it to BROTHER JASPER.

PRESIDENT. Brother Jasper, you will be our ultimate guarantee that however this war will be decided, the infernal powers will not prevail. Find Lyra and kill her.

BROTHER JASPER. Thank you.

PRESIDENT. I thank *you*. How much better it would be for us all if there had been a Brother Jasper in the Garden of Eden! We would never have left paradise.

They go.

A faltering message is seen / heard from LORD ROKE.

LORD ROKE. *Roke here . . . gravest danger . . . Lyra and Will are expected to leave the dead zone . . . the assassin will find them once they have entered the living world . . . the Clouded Mountain has set forth and will be visible from your fortress shortly . . . on a personal note, regret return impossible . . . I am proud to have served Your Lordship . . . losing the light . . .*

The Land of the Dead. NO-NAME *flies ahead.* LYRA, WILL *and* ROGER *follow her lead, at the head of a winding trail of ghosts.*

LYRA. Is it much further, No-Name?

NO-NAME. Just follow. If you can't see, listen. If you can't hear, feel.

The abyss appears.

WILL. Lyra! Look at that.

LYRA. What is it?

JOPARI. It's the darkest secret of the underworld. When the first rebellion of the angels was defeated, the Authority sentenced its leader to something worse than death. He opened up this endless abyss and cast him into it, to fall for eternity. Ever since then, the abyss has continued its evil work.

Golden light appears, streaming downwards.

Do you see that golden light? It's Dust from all the worlds, being sucked into blackness and lost for ever.

WILL *and* LYRA *look down it.*

LYRA. Can you see to the bottom, Will?

WILL. Looks like it goes down forever. I don't like it. Something bad's gonna happen.

LYRA *moves nearer to the edge.*

JOPARI. Careful, Lyra! If you fall, you'll fall for the rest of your life.

LYRA. That wouldn't be long though, would it? 'Cause I'd die of starvation. We can walk round the edge of it, look.

She walks precariously along the edge. The GHOSTS *call out to her to be careful.*

Remember, Rodge, how you an' me used to climb on the roof at Jordan? And I dared you to stand on the top of a drainpipe, an' you . . .

She slips and falls into the abyss. The GHOSTS *scream in terror.*

WILL. Lyra!

NO-NAME. Make way!

NO-NAME *spreads her wings, flies down towards* LYRA *and lifts her back to safety.*

LYRA. Oh, No-Name! Thank you! Thank you!

ROGER (*calls*). Lyra! Look up there! There's daylight!

There's a ripple of excitement from the GHOSTS, *as they all climb on.*

LORD ASRIEL*'s fortress.* OFFICERS *are looking out from the ramparts.*

1ST OFFICER. It's there! The Clouded Mountain!

2ND OFFICER. It's getting closer!

3RD OFFICER. Sound the alarm!

LORD ASRIEL *appears below.*

LORD ASRIEL. Are our troops on the ground in place?

4TH OFFICER. They are, My Lord.

LORD ASRIEL. And the angel-battalions?

5TH OFFICER. They're standing by.

OFFICERS *cross the battlefield from left and right, calling.*

OFFICERS. Stand by for the signal! / Get ready! / Sound the alert!

MRS COULTER *appears.*

MRS COULTER. Asriel!

LORD ASRIEL. Quick, tell me. What have you learned?

MRS COULTER. Her name is Eve.

LORD ASRIEL. *Eve?* Then you were right, Marisa. She *is*
unique. If she survives what lies ahead of her, she'll do all
that I hoped to do myself. She'll smash the universe to
pieces and she'll put it together in her own way.

4TH OFFICER. My Lord, it's gathering speed. Will you give
the order?

LORD ASRIEL. Let it come closer.

They look up at the Clouded Mountain.

Somewhere inside that terrifying mass is a crystal casket.
And there the Authority lies. The angel-tyrant that I've
sworn to destroy. And I don't have the knife, and I doubt
that I ever shall. But there's something we possess that is
just as powerful. It's this.

He touches her.

Our flesh. The angels long to have bodies like ours, so real,
so strong, so firmly planted on the good earth. And if we
use that power, if we're determined, we can brush them
away like smoke!

He turns to the army around him.

Friends! This is the last rebellion and the best. Never before
have angels and humans, and beings from all the worlds and
the power of nature itself made common cause to build a
world where there aren't any kingdoms at all. No kings, no
bishops, no priests. We'll be free citizens of the Republic of
Heaven.

He gives the signal.

*The mouth of the Land of the Dead. NO-NAME looks out.
LYRA and WILL look out after her.*

WILL. Just breathe.

LYRA. Amazing.

NO-NAME. Have you no thanks for me?

LYRA. Yeah, I do. You saved my life. And you brought us
here, and you'll bring the ghosts up here for ever after. And
if you en't got a name, that can't be right for a job that's so
important. Iorek Byrnison called me 'Lyra Silvertongue' . . .
and I'm giving a name to you. I'll call you 'Gracious
Wings'.

NO-NAME. I will see you again, Lyra Silvertongue.

LYRA. And when you do, Gracious Wings, I won't be afraid.
Goodbye.

She kisses GRACIOUS WINGS, *who goes back into the
Land of the Dead.* ROGER *comes out, calling to the
GHOSTS behind him.*

ROGER. I wanna go first. The rest of you, wait your turn. (*To
LYRA.*) It will be all right, won't it?

LYRA. Yeah.

ROGER. I'll be part of the wind and the sun, just like Will's
dad was saying?

LYRA. I'm sure of it, Rodge. And when I die, I'll be a part
of it with you.

ROGER. That's good. That's *wonderful*, Lyra. (*To the
GHOSTS behind him.*) Come on!

He disappears along with other GHOSTS *beside him.*
JOPARI *appears.*

JOPARI. In a moment, Will, you'll go through to the
battlefield. But there's something that I must say to you
first, and Lyra too. When I left my world, I was as healthy
and strong as a man could be. Twelve years later I was
dying. Do you understand what that means? We can only
survive in the world that we're born in. Lord Asriel's war
will fail for the same reason. We must build the Republic of
Heaven where we are. Because for us, there's no elsewhere.

WILL. I've got something to say to you too. You said I was a
warrior. You said it was in my nature, and I shouldn't argue.
Well, you were wrong. My nature's what it is, and maybe
I can't change that. But I can choose what I do. And I will.

JOHN PARRY. Well done, my son. I'm proud of you. No one on earth could have done better than this. Now go. Cut your window.

He disappears. WILL *cuts a window into . . .*

. . . the battlefield. Immediate noise and confusion. FIGHTERS *from both sides advance and retreat.* BROTHER JASPER *is seen with his rifle, stalking through the mêlée.* IOREK *appears and attacks him.* JASPER'*s quickness and agility in the fight make* IOREK *look slow and clumsy.* BROTHER JASPER *fires, wounding* IOREK *and runs out of sight, wounded himself.* LYRA *and* WILL *run on.*

LYRA. Iorek!

IOREK. Lyra Silvertongue! And Will!

LYRA. You're wounded!

IOREK. It was the priest, the priest with the rifle. Get away from the battlefield. Leave at once. He's come to kill you.

WILL. He can't do a thing. I've got the knife.

IOREK. He has the symbol-reader, Will! He can outwit the knife! He even outwitted me. Run, quick as you can!

WILL. You don't understand. I've got to find Lord Asriel, like I promised!

IOREK. Then you must keep your promise. I'll find the priest, and do what I can to hold him back. If I survive, you children will always be welcome at Svalbard.

LYRA. Won't you go back to the mountains?

IOREK. No, my child. I was mistaken. My bears can't live in those snows. We must return to my ruined kingdom, and make what lives we can. Go well.

LYRA. Go well, King Iorek.

IOREK *cuffs* WILL *gently and goes.*

WILL. Come on, let's go.

LYRA sees the Authority's crystal casket, lying where it fell on the battlefield.

LYRA. Hang on. What's that?

WILL. Dunno.

LYRA. Let's go and look.

WILL. Lyra!

LYRA. It won't take a minute.

She goes and looks into it.

Will! There's a man inside.

WILL goes and looks.

WILL. That isn't a man. He's an angel, like Baruch and Balthamos, only . . . incredibly old.

LYRA. I never seen anyone so old.

WILL. He looks like one more breath'd be too much effort.

LYRA. Look how he's scrabbling his fingers.

WILL. He's crying.

LYRA. It's horrible. Can't we do summing to help him?

WILL. Yeah, 'course we can. I'll cut him out.

He cuts the casket open and reaches in to lift the Authority out.

LYRA. Don't touch him!

WILL. Why?

LYRA. 'Cause something's happening.

WILL. Yeah! It is!

LYRA. You opened the top, an' the air rushed in an' touched his face an' . . .

WILL. He's getting fainter.

LYRA. Like smoke.

WILL. Like smoke dissolving.

LYRA. He's smiling, look.

WILL. He is!

LYRA. 'Cause he's so glad to be dying! I can still see him
a bit, can you?

WILL. Yeah, just a flicker.

They watch.

Still smiling.

They watch.

LYRA. He's gone.

WILL *starts to go.*

WILL. We can't hang about.

LYRA. No, not if that priest is after us.

WILL. Not just that! I gotta take this knife to your dad, so he
can kill the Authority!

LYRA. You're right. Let's go.

They go. SOLDIERS *of* LORD ASRIEL'*s army run on.*

SOLDIERS. I saw it! / Over here! / Lord Asriel! / It's the
crystal casket! / It's the Authority!

LORD ASRIEL *appears.*

LORD ASRIEL. How did it happen?

1ST SOLDIER. I saw it all, My Lord. The Clouded Mountain
sounded the retreat. I looked up, and there were four enemy
angels flying away from it with something sparkling in their
hands. The rebels attacked them, and it fell to earth. The
Authority's there, inside that casket.

LORD ASRIEL *goes to the casket and looks into it.*

LORD ASRIEL. It's empty.

SOLDIERS. It can't be! / It was locked! / We saw him!

SERAFINA *appears.*

SERAFINA. The children have freed him. But they're still on the battlefield and their assassin has nearly found them. Lord Asriel, you know what you have to do. I beg you, do it. All, all depends on the next few moments.

MRS COULTER *is heard calling.*

MRS COULTER. Asriel!

SERAFINA. It's the woman who killed my witches. If I see her, I won't be able to let her live. Farewell.

She goes.

LORD ASRIEL. Go, all of you.

The SOLDIERS *go.* MRS COULTER *appears.*

MRS COULTER. Have you seen Lyra?

LORD ASRIEL. She's very near. So is your little priest. You must stop him, Marisa. You're the only person who can do it. Lyra must live. That's all that matters.

MRS COULTER. What about your Republic?

LORD ASRIEL. It's here! It's now! The knife did what it was meant to do, and the Authority's gone. But there's only one reason for my Republic to exist. It's to prepare the world for Lyra.

MRS COULTER. So we must save her at the cost of everything? Even our lives?

LORD ASRIEL. Those most of all.

MRS COULTER. So . . . just as Adam and Eve replenished the world with Dust . . . our children will do the same, in whatever Garden of Eden they find. And if they can't . . .

LORD ASRIEL. . . . then it isn't our world to worry about. Our part is over.

The abyss appears.

MRS COULTER. What is it?

LORD ASRIEL. It's the end I dreamed of. It's the abyss.

WILL is heard calling.

WILL. Lord Asriel!

LORD ASRIEL. Don't let them see you.

MRS COULTER. But she must know what we're doing!

LORD ASRIEL. No! She'd feel a burden of guilt at the very moment when she needs to be free. When she's older, she'll look back at it all. And then she'll know. Stand back.

They do. WILL *comes running on, full tilt.* LYRA *follows him.*

WILL. Lord Asriel! (*To* LYRA.) He must be somewhere!

LYRA. He'd find us, wouldn't he, if he wanted to? So would my mum. And listen. It's all gone quiet. The battle's over.

MRS COULTER *is about to speak.* LORD ASRIEL *signals to her to be quiet. Unseen by the others,* BROTHER JASPER *appears. He aims his rifle at* LYRA.

Everyone's gone. Your dad. Serafina. Iorek, so old and powerless. It's all coming on to us now.

WILL. Yeah . . . we gotta look after ourselves.

LYRA. And find someplace where we can't get killed.

WILL. I'll cut a window.

He does. BROTHER JASPER *is about to fire. Unseen by the children,* MRS COULTER *steps forward where* BROTHER JASPER *can see her. She whispers fiercely.*

MRS COULTER. Jasper!

He stares at her. LYRA *and* WILL *go through the window and it closes behind them.* BROTHER JASPER *laughs.*

BROTHER JASPER. They won't get away! There are windows everywhere. I know them all.

MRS COULTER. Jasper, look at me. What do you see?

BROTHER JASPER. Sin. Corruption.

MRS COULTER. Touch it. You wanted to, from the moment you saw me.

She kisses him. Unseen by BROTHER JASPER, LORD ASRIEL *moves towards them.*

Come with me, and you can touch it until you die. We'll fall forever, like the brightest and best of angels.

He pulls away from her.

BROTHER JASPER. No.

LORD ASRIEL *seizes his hand.* MRS COULTER *seizes the other.*

No! No!

LORD ASRIEL *and* MRS COULTER *leap into the abyss, taking* BROTHER JASPER *with them.*

An unknown world. LYRA *and* WILL *are sitting on the ground. A bowl of hedge-fruit is between them.* LYRA *picks one up.*

LYRA. It's true what Roger said. You know at once when you like somebody. And I liked you.

WILL. That night on the mountain . . . you were asleep . . . and I said to Pan that you were the best friend I'd ever had.

LYRA. I heard you. I was lying awake!

WILL. That's funny. 'Cause when Serafina was talking about the blackberries, I was lying awake as well.

LYRA. When you said that to Pan, I wanted to sit up and say all the same things to you. Then your father died, because he wouldn't be unfaithful to your mother. You'd be like that.

She crushes a blackberry against his mouth.

I love you, Will.

They kiss.

An unknown world. SERAFINA *looks through her amber spyglass.*

SERAFINA. The moon is high. But the clouds are still. Two children are lying in each other's arms in an unknown world. I look through the amber spyglass and I see a change. Dust is moving differently . . . there's a current here, a swirl of it there . . . all falling like rain on the poor parched throat of the earth. Life has returned. The world is renewed. The Dust pouring down from the stars has found its living home . . . and those two young children . . . no longer children . . . have made it happen.

Same world. Morning. WILL *and* LYRA *are asleep, their arms around each other.* PANTALAIMON *and* WILL*'s daemon,* KIRJAVA, *join them, both as cats.* LYRA *wakes and sees them.*

LYRA. Pan! Oh Pan, you're back!

PANTALAIMON. I thought I'd never, ever find you.

LYRA *embraces him.* WILL *wakes up and sees* KIRJAVA.

WILL. Hey, what's this?

PANTALAIMON. What does it look like?

WILL. Is it my daemon? Is it? Honest?

KIRJAVA. Pick me up.

WILL *does.*

WILL. Hello.

KIRJAVA. Hello.

WILL. I'll have to give her a name.

SERAFINA *is there.*

SERAFINA. I've done that already.

KIRJAVA. My name is Kirjava.

SERAFINA. Her shape has settled, I think.

LYRA. And Pan?

PANTALAIMON. I've settled too.

LYRA. You're so beautiful. I can't believe that I got so used to being without you.

SERAFINA. What you did, without knowing it, was what we witches have always done. It's painful for us, but once that's over, we and our daemons can wander free. So can you. You will always be one whole being, even when you are apart.

The DAEMONS *spring from* LYRA's *and* WILL's *arms and crouch sadly at a distance from them.*

LYRA. Then why are they suddenly so sad?

SERAFINA. Because they know what I have to tell you.

LYRA. What?

SERAFINA. The worlds were dying. Dust was flowing away, sucked in by that great abyss in the underworld. Only you could save it. (*To* LYRA.) This was your destiny, Lyra. To be true to your secret name. You were tempted and fell, and so the Triumph of Dust began. But it isn't complete. Dust continues to flow away, and all that is good will die unless you stop it.

LYRA. *How* is it flowing?

WILL. I think I know.

SERAFINA. Dust escapes every time a window is left open, as though from a wound that goes on bleeding.

WILL. You mean that the windows must all be closed?

SERAFINA. They will be. It's a task for the angels.

WILL. Then Lyra and me, we just gotta close our windows after we've made them. That'll be all right, won't it?

SERAFINA. No. Every time you cut a window, it makes a Spectre. That's why Cittàgazze was so full of Spectres, because there are so many windows there.

LYRA. We can't make Spectres, Will. We gotta cut no more windows.

WILL. But Lyra and me are from different worlds. If I can't cut a window, then we . . .

He realises what he's saying.

. . . then we won't ever see each other. There's got to be *one*.

SERAFINA. One is allowed.

WILL. For us?

LYRA. No. Not for us. It's for the dead to escape by, isn't it? We can't take that away from them.

WILL. No, we can't.

LYRA. But that don't matter. You and me can live in the same world, Will! It'll have to be yours, 'cause you can't leave your mother. But I got nobody now. I'll live with you.

WILL. No! Don't you remember what my dad said? 'We can only survive in the world that we're born in.' That's why he was dying.

LYRA. I don't care. I'll be happy to die, just so long as we're together.

WILL. Do you think I could bear that? To see you getting sicker and sicker, while I got stronger and more grown-up every day? Do you think I could live on after you died? No, never, never.

LYRA. We can't leave each other, Will. There must be a way! I know! I'll ask the alethiometer. It's bound to know.

She turns the wheels. Stares at it.

It isn't working. What's the matter with it?

SERAFINA. Nothing's the matter. You've lost the childlike grace that made you able to read it. And you'll never be able to read it again in the way you did. But there's a different grace that comes with study. Work hard, and the time will come when you read it more deeply than ever.

Will, you and Lyra must go into your world now. There'll
be an angel there, who you must teach to close the
windows. Then you will cut your final window. You and
Lyra will say farewell. Then you must break the knife.

The Botanic Gardens in WILL*'s world.* KIRJAVA *has stayed
behind with* SERAFINA.

LYRA. I want to kiss you and lie down with you . . . and sleep
. . . and wake up with you every day of my life until I die.

WILL. I'll always love you. And when I die, I'll drift about
forever, all my atoms, till they mix with yours.

LYRA. Every atom of you, every atom of me.

Pause.

WILL. It's time.

LYRA. Come on, Pan.

She picks up PANTALAIMON.

If we meet someone that we like, later on, we gotta be good
to them, and not make comparisons. But . . . Once a year . . .
just once a year . . . We could both come here, to the
Botanic Gardens, on Midsummer Night at midnight . . . And
talk till dawn, just like now, as though we were together
again. Because we *will* be.

WILL. I will. I promise. Wherever I am in the world, I'll come
back here.

LYRA. At midnight.

WILL. Till the following dawn.

LYRA. For as long as I live.

WILL. For as long as I live.

He cuts a window.

LYRA. Goodbye.

WILL. Goodbye.

> LYRA *goes through. They stand looking at each other.*
> BALTHAMOS *is there.*

BALTHAMOS. Now you must close it.

LYRA. Close it.

> WILL *closes the window.* LYRA *turns away in tears.*

BALTHAMOS. It will be the work of a lifetime to close them all. But one must do what's right, even after you have lost the one you love. Now break the knife.

> WILL *extends the knife into the air.*

WILL. How?

BALTHAMOS. Do as you did before. Think of whatever is most important to you. Then try to cut.

WILL. Lyra.

> *The knife shatters.*

Dawn breaks. We're in the present day.

WILL. I wanted to go through after you.

LYRA. I wanted to stay.

WILL. But then I remembered what my dad said. There's no elsewhere . . .

LYRA. You must be where you are . . .

WILL. . . . and where you are is the place that matters most of all . . .

LYRA. . . . 'cause it's the only place where you can make . . .

WILL. . . . where you can build . . .

LYRA. . . . where you can share . . .

WILL. . . . what you've been looking for all along . . .

LYRA. The Republic of Heaven.

Two clocks are heard striking. LYRA *picks up*
PANTALAIMON. *She and* WILL *pass each other and walk
out of sight.*

End of Part Two.

Production Note

This adaptation was written to be played in the National Theatre's Olivier Theatre, making maximum use of that seldom-seen, subterranean monster, the Olivier's drum-revolve. The demands and abilities of this mighty piece of '70s technology are now inseparable from the script. But I like to think that the adaptation – though it was written for a theatre with vast resources – could have a different kind of life in productions that have no resources at all. The fantastic demands of Pullman's imagination can be fulfilled in many different ways, and there's plenty in the books themselves to stir the imagination. The important thing is that the story moves swiftly from scene to scene.